B+T
$6.95

TWAYNE'S
RULERS AND STATESMEN OF THE WORLD
SERIES

Hans L. Trefousse, Brooklyn College
General Editor

LENIN

(TROW 21)

Lenin

By ROBERT D. WARTH

University of Kentucky

Twayne Publishers, Inc. :: New York

LIBRARY OF CONGRESS CATALOG CARD NUMBER: 73-1760

ISBN–0–8057–3055–9
MANUFACTURED IN THE UNITED STATES OF AMERICA

Preface

The modern world has produced no more seminal a figure than Lenin. His life, indissoluble from the birth of Communism, the Russian Revolution, and the beginnings of the Soviet state, has attracted numerous biographers and other chroniclers of Russia's revolutionary history. The Lenin cult, never more pervasive in his homeland than it is today, continues to disgorge a staggering volume of Leniniana, almost all of it worthless to the serious scholar. In the West the Lenin mystique enjoys no official recognition, and the market place of ideas is receptive to a variety of interpretations, most of them written with non-Communist if not anti-Communist premises and therefore at least implicitly critical of Lenin.

Despite the proliferation of Lenin studies, there is no "standard" life of the man, nor is there a satisfactory short biography that combines scholarship with readability. Although it has no novel "thesis" to present, this work seeks to fulfill that need. Perfect objectivity is an impossible goal, but I have tried to present a controversial subject in a nonpartisan spirit. Hagiography seems to me a poor way of perpetuating Lenin's memory. At the other extreme, I do not share the view that he was simply the "Red dictator" who prepared the way for Stalin's totalitarian regime.

Lenin spent much of his life abroad. To avoid shifting back and forth between the old style calendar (used in Russia until February 1918) and the Western calendar, all dates are given according to the latter.

I am grateful to Mrs. Natalie Schick for deciphering a handwritten manuscript and transforming it into typewritten copy.

Contents

LENIN

CHAPTER I

To the Finland Station

VLADIMIR ILYICH ULYANOV (N. LENIN), THE FOUNDER OF BOLSHE-vism, later to be renamed Communism, accepted without question the Marxist premise of the inevitable downfall of capitalism. Although the immediate prospect seemed discouraging, "We must not be deceived by the present grave-like stillness," he told an audience of youthful sympathizers in Zurich, Switzerland, on January 22, 1917, for "Europe is pregnant with revolution." Yet even he, whose orthodoxy was second to none, suffered minor lapses of faith, and he concluded his speech lamely by confessing that "we of the older generation may not live to see the decisive battles of this coming revolution."[1]

If Europe was not precisely "pregnant" with revolution, the Russian empire was. "The monstrous horrors of the imperialist war" (to borrow Lenin's phrase) had undermined the foundations of habit, tradition, and popular loyalty that had kept the Romanov dynasty in power since 1613 and Nicholas II on the throne since 1894. Less than two months elapsed from the time of Lenin's pessimistic appraisal to the overthrow of the Tsar. To the Bolsheviks, as to other professional revolutionaries, the news came as a startling surprise. Generations of agitators, publicists, and assorted critics of the tsarist system had predicted revolution, but even the most astute observers were taken unaware when their theoretical extrapolations were borne out by actual events. The anonymous masses, particularly the workers and soldiers of Petrograd (St. Petersburg until 1914), erupted with a spontaneity and unanimity rare in the annals of political upheaval. A committee of the State Duma (the legislative assembly now technically dissolved), with no satisfactory credentials from the populace, stepped into the political vacuum to choose a new government. Composed of "liberals"—and one nominal socialist—who shared the values of Western parliamentary democracy, the cabinet formally assumed office on March 16. It was headed by Prince Georgi Lvov, a colorless but respected public figure whose subsequent career revealed him to be little more than a figurehead for more dominant personalities.

Nearly all of Russia's revolutionary leaders were either abroad or in Siberian exile. Lenin had lived in Switzerland since 1914, and the winter just ending had not been a cheerful one. Depressed and nervous, he was also in financial difficulty, reduced to seeking assignments as a translator and planning (with his wife's assistance) a pedagogical encyclopedia. Nor had his own political battles—a melancholy commentary on the realities of émigré life—been going well. "There it is, my fate," he complained in a letter to his friend Inessa Armand. "One fighting campaign after another—against political nonsense, philistinism, opportunism, etc."[2] Now that the climactic event about which his whole being revolved had actually occurred, he was frantic with impatience to get to the scene of the action. "What torture it is," he wrote to an old associate in Stockholm, "for us all to sit here at such a time!"[3] But the logistics of returning to his homeland were not easily solved. The Allied powers could not be expected to facilitate the journey of avowed opponents of the war, and to the Central powers Russian citizens were enemy aliens. Neither was the Provisional Government, as the self-appointed successor of the tsarist regime called itself, eager to welcome those whose political views clashed with the bourgeois assumptions of the new leadership and the comfortable illusion that Russia could "wage a war and manage a revolution at the same time" (to use the words of Mikhail Rodzyanko, the last president of the Duma). The new democratic Russia did grant a sweeping amnesty to political offenders but proved stubbornly resistant to the idea of carrying out its own mandate when anti-war radicals of Lenin's persuasion sought to redeem the pledge. Luckily for them, the Petrograd Soviet, representing the workers and soldiers of the capital and exercising quasi-governmental functions with impunity, blocked discriminatory measures against the Bolsheviks and other spokesmen of the extreme Left.

Lenin soon discarded his more fanciful schemes of returning to Russia—using a false Swedish passport, for example, and disguising his ignorance of the language by posing as a deaf mute. The route through Germany seemed the most feasible, for the

Kaiser's government—like the other belligerents—was willing to use any available weapon, political as well as military, to win the war. But the negotiations were delicate and time-consuming. Meanwhile, though continually chafing at the delay, Lenin busied himself with a series of "Letters from Afar" analyzing Russian developments from the scanty press reports available in Switzerland. Only the first appeared in *Pravda*, the chief Bolshevik organ, and three others were apparently rejected as badly dated and ill-informed. A Bolshevik intermediary, Alexandra Kollontai, had received them in Christiania (now Oslo) and personally delivered them on April 1. The new editorial board, headed by Joseph Stalin and Leo Kamenev (they had just returned from Siberia) demonstrated sound judgment. Even the first letter assumed, without a shred of evidence, that the Tsar had been deposed by an Anglo-French conspiracy in conjunction with various bourgeois leaders "for the purpose of continuing the imperialist war." Ironically, variations of this theme were widely accepted in right-wing circles: many politically naive monarchists continued to believe in the reality of a plot hatched in the British and French embassies, and not a few leaders of the Provisional Government, who should have known better, deluded themselves that the March Revolution had been a mass protest against the inefficient conduct of the war. But however misguided his views, Lenin made it clear that he rejected collaboration with the "landlord and capitalist government." Stalin and the Bolshevik leadership on the spot drifted toward "conciliationism," baffled by a situation that had not been foreseen in the Marxist handbooks and uncertain what the party's course ought to be.

Although it would be a slight exaggeration to say that Lenin was unknown on the eve of his departure for Russia, he was certainly a political cipher to the European public, including otherwise well informed Russians who lacked specific knowledge of the revolutionary movement. In March, 1917, well before the occult chemistry of world fame catapulted him from an obscure exile to a living legend, he was just short of his forty-seventh birthday. A rather stocky man of slightly less than average height, he dressed conservatively, lived frugally, and avoided the temperamental mannerisms and erratic habits so typical (at least in the popular image) of revolutionaries. Nor did he enjoy those endless Russian "socials" in which political debate combined with gossip and idle chatter to help fill the void of émigré existence. Except for his ideas, which "respectable" citizens would have found shocking, there was little to distinguish him from a provincial lawyer (his occupation at one time) or a petty tradesman. Nearly bald, his remaining hair, including a neat mustache and beard, was faintly red, and his oval face, with tiny eyes and a high forehead and cheekbones, bore traces of Mongolian ancestry. While genial and unpretentious—possessed also of humor, charm, and courtesy—he was often intolerant and dogmatic in political controversy, allowing personal friendships to stand or fall on the basis of doctrinal purity and revolutionary strategy. His will power and self-discipline were awesome, yet the seeming ease with which he controlled his emotions concealed an undercurrent of nervous tension that sometimes left him ill and exhausted after a particularly trying confrontation. Compared to politics, he cared little for art, literature, and music, though he admired the Russian literary classics and confessed to the writer Maxim Gorky, after hearing a Beethoven sonata: "It is marvelous superhuman music. I always think with pride—perhaps it is naive of me—what marvelous things human beings can do!" Then, smiling and characteristically screwing up his eyes, he added rather sadly: "But I can't listen to music too often. It affects your nerves, makes you want to say stupid, nice things, and stroke the heads of people who could create such beauty while living in this vile hell."[4] Lenin had no hobbies or avocation other than reading, while chess, the favorite recreation of his youth, was virtually abandoned upon his return to Russia because it tired rather than refreshed him.

Unknown to Lenin, the German government had already taken an interest in his case. Its key informant was Alexander Helphand, a versatile German Social Democrat better known as Parvus, who had a wide acquaintance among the Russian revolutionaries, Lenin included. Helphand's emissary, Georg Sklarz, contacted Lenin in Zurich, but his status as a German agent was so obvious that Lenin felt constrained to decline his offer of an unhindered passage across Germany free of charge. Another channel for negotiations was soon found: Fritz Platten, the secretary of the Swiss Socialist Party, arranged the details of the projected journey with the German minister in Berne, who on

April 2, 1917, was advised by his superiors in Berlin to expedite matters since the Allied powers had begun to pressure the Swiss authorities. The trip had already received the approval of the German General Staff. The substance of the agreement provided that the Russian émigrés would be allowed passage regardless of their political views or attitude toward the war; that Platten would act as courier and that no one would be allowed to enter their private railway car without his permission; that they would be granted extraterritorial rights, including freedom from inspection of passports and luggage; and that the passengers would agitate in Russia for the repatriation of an equal number of German and Austrian war prisoners or internees.

By the second week in April arrangements had been completed with the German government to transport Lenin and his party from Switzerland to Sweden in what came to be called, with gross inaccuracy, the "sealed train." Much nonsense was written in 1917 and thereafter exposing Lenin (and the Bolshevik leaders generally) as a "German agent," presumably a paid employee who could be counted on the carry out whatever instructions he received from Berlin. Such charges usually stemmed from his political opponents or from Allied officials and propagandists who knew little or nothing about either Lenin or Bolshevism. That a man of his single-minded dedication to the revolutionary cause would be subverted by money or favors was inconceivable. But he was undeniably an opportunist and quite without scruples when the needs of the movement were at stake. For the moment the mutual interests of the party and the German government coincided. That such an interest (at least on Berlin's part) arose suddenly in the spring of 1917 is disproved by a meager but significant collection of documents from the German Foreign Office published after World War II.[5] They demonstrate that considerable effort and sizable sums of money were expended to contact and support the political enemies of the tsarist regime. But these financial transactions were invariably made through intermediaries, and there is no evidence presently available (though such may exist in Soviet archives) proving conclusively that the Bolsheviks ever received a penny of German money. We may reasonably surmise, however, that the go-betweens did not invariably extract one hundred percent commissions for their services, nor need we assume that Lenin was unaware of the source of the funds that were presumably siphoned into the party coffers. It may be that he was careful to look the other way so that his later protestations that he was unsullied by the taint of "German gold" were technically accurate. Just when these clandestine payments began is uncertain, but it is improbable that the party received any funds before the March Revolution because of the straitened circumstances of Lenin and his associates in Switzerland. Once in power the following November the German subsidy was no longer necessary, although it is probable that the ties were broken several months earlier when the Provisional Government publicized the German agent charge.

When word came that Platten's negotiations were successful, Lenin decided to leave at once. Within two hours he and his wife wound up their affairs—personal belongings packed, books returned to the library, letters destroyed, and the landlady paid. The emigrants, thirty-two in all, gathered at the People's House in Zurich. Nineteen, according to later Soviet accounts, were Bolsheviks, of whom Gregory Zinoviev, Karl Radek, Inessa Armand, and Gregory Sokolnikov were the best known aside from Lenin himself. After a farewell luncheon, at which Lenin read the draft of a "letter" to the Swiss workers, the revolutionaries left for the railway station. A few hostile demonstrators were on hand, but except for an exchange of angry taunts the passengers boarded the train without incident. Lenin is said to have evicted a suspected Okhrana (tsarist secret police) agent who tried to join the party.

The train departed on the afternoon of April 9. At the German frontier the Russians were assigned a separate coach in which three of the four doors were locked. Two German officers were installed in the last compartment—watchdogs of the high command—and a chalk line drawn across the corridor as a Russo-German boundary. At Stuttgart, Wilhelm Jansson, a labor union executive apparently sent by Helphand, sought to meet the Bolsheviks but was rebuffed by Platten on Lenin's instructions. The passengers were well fed and enjoyed such high priority that the authorities held up a train carrying the German crown prince for two hours. Yet delays were normal in wartime: Frankfurt proved to be a bottleneck, and in Berlin the train was shunted to a siding and remained overnight. Whether the Russians left their coach or met German representatives is not known, but it seems unlikely that Lenin would have risked compromising himself. Not a word of the unorthodox journey leaked into the press, apparently because of tight security rather than voluntary or imposed censorship.

The train left Berlin on the morning of April 12 and reached the Baltic coast in the afternoon. The passengers transferred to a Swedish cargo vessel which safely negotiated mine fields to the port of Trelleborg in Sweden. There they entrained for Stockholm and spent most of the day there—the thirteenth. Lenin conferred with a number of Swedish socialists and attended a banquet for the returning Russians. He also saw a good deal of Jacob Fürstenberg (known as Ganetsky in Russian and Hanecki in German), a Polish Social Democrat and a Bolshevik agent who had joined him at Trelleborg for the trip to Stockholm. But he avoided a personal meeting with Helphand as politically dangerous, and Radek, barred from Russia because of his Austrian citizenship, remained closeted with Helphand for many hours. The presumption is strong that the subject of conversation involved German support for the Bolsheviks. "It is unlikely," as Helphand's biographers wryly observe, "that they spent much time discussing Marxist theories."[6]

A number of Swedish socialists signed a document approving the Bolsheviks' passage through Germany and contributed to a fund to help defray their expenses. The Swedish foreign minister, asked for a donation, is said to have replied: "Gladly, so long as Lenin leaves today."[7] The emigrants did indeed resume their northward journey that evening, and on April 15 they transferred from a train to horse-drawn sleighs to cross the Finnish border at Tornio. British officers were stationed at the frontier post—how they happened to be on duty there is not clear—and Lenin was supposedly taken to a separate room and subjected to a humiliating search. Platten, as a Swiss national, was turned back. At last, on board a Russian train (Finland was then an archduchy within the empire), Lenin was able to obtain recent editions of the Petrograd newspapers and to familiarize himself with the political climate of his homeland—a formidable assignment when he had had only the haphazard accounts available in the Swiss, German, and Swedish press. He was still concerned about the possibility of arrest once he reached the capital. At Byelo-Ostrov, on the Russian border, a delegation of workers and prominent Bolsheviks met the train, and Lenin made a short speech at the station. His sister Maria, Kamenev (whom Lenin scolded without rancor for the tone of his *Pravda* editorials), and other party members joined him for the short ride into Petrograd. He arrived at the Finland Station late in the evening of April 16.

CHAPTER II

The Young Revolutionary

LENIN WAS BORN ON APRIL 22, 1870, IN THE SLEEPY PROVINCIAL CITY of Simbirsk (now Ulyanovsk) on the upper Volga. His father, Ilya Ulyanov, a graduate of Kazan University, had pursued a teaching career in mathematics and physics and became inspector of schools in the Simbirsk area several months before his son Vladimir's birth. He was later promoted to director of schools for the province, a civil service rank (equivalent to a major general in the army) that automatically conferred on him the status of hereditary nobleman. A dedicated pedagogue and educational administrator, he never, so far as is known, wavered in his loyalty to the tsarist regime despite Soviet insinuations that he was at least a revolutionary sympathizer. Lenin's mother, Maria Blank before her marriage, was the daughter of a somewhat eccentric physician and landowner and had been educated by tutors. Young Vladimir—or Volodya as he was usually called as an affectionate diminutive—grew up in relatively affluent surroundings, a background that Soviet historians tend to ignore or to minimize as unseemly for a great proletarian hero. Even more embarrassing to a regime that prefers to think of its founding father as an ethnically pure Russian, Lenin's maternal grandmother was German in origin and his paternal grandmother was of Kalmuck ancestry. (The Kalmucks were a Mongolian people of Buddhist faith who settled in the area north of the Caspian Sea.) Lenin's childhood was normal, even idyllic, if one may judge solely from family memoirs, a genre that tends toward filial piety and, in this case, fraternal loyalty overladen with the sanctity of the Leninist cult. Naturally bright and energetic, he was studious, disciplined, and highly motivated but displayed none of that irritating precociousness that usually denotes ambitious parents rather than a child prodigy. He was tutored at home until he

[21]

entered the local *gymnasium* (high school) at the early age of
nine and a half. The curriculum was demanding, but his grades
were excellent, and there is no evidence that he took an interest
in politics or manifested any unconventionality of behavior or
ideas. One exception may be noted: at the age of sixteen he became an atheist, or so he stated in a party questionnaire many
years later. The "official" Soviet version of his break with the
church—obviously apocryphal—is at least dramatic. A guest is
supposed to have pointed out to Ilya Ulyanov that his children
were poor churchgoers and remarked, looking directly at Vladimir, "Give him the birch, don't spare it!" The boy ran out of
the house and angrily tore off the cross he wore around his neck.[1]

Two events marred the outward serenity of Vladimir's adoles-
cence. His father died suddenly in 1886, and fourteen months
later his older brother Alexander, a student at St. Petersburg
University, was hanged for his part in an amateurish plot against
the life of Tsar Alexander III. Of the two tragedies, the death of
his brother seems to have left a far greater emotional scar. His
Soviet biographers uphold the legend that Lenin, hearing the
news, said to his sister Maria (who relates the incident in her
memoirs) : "No, we won't take that path. That isn't the path to
take."[2] The implication is that he had already become a Marxist
and rejected the revolutionary terrorism of the Narodniks (Populists) as faulty political strategy. That was far from the case, but
the circumstances of Alexander's death could not fail to sharpen
Lenin's nascent political consciousness.

The Ulyanov family, shunned by polite society in Simbirsk,
closed ranks in the face of misfortune. Demonstrating remarkable self-control, Vladimir completed his studies at the *gymnasium*
shortly after the execution and won the coveted gold medal as
the best student in the graduating class. The school's principal,
Fyodor Kerensky (by a curious coincidence the father of Alexander Kerensky, whose government the Bolsheviks were to overthrow in the October Revolution), courageously gave him a
glowing recommendation, and he enrolled in the law faculty of
Kazan University in the fall of 1887. Although lacking the prestige
of the older universities of Moscow and St. Petersburg, Kazan
was by no means a second-rate institution. The city itself, some
150 miles upriver from Simbirsk and the historic capital of one
of the medieval Tartar Khanates, was larger and more cosmopoli-

tan than Vladimir's home town. His family, including a brother and three sisters, moved to Kazan during the summer. His mother's pension and other assets, including the sale of the house in Simbirsk and a small estate near Kazan inherited from her father, provided a meager but not uncomfortable livelihood in the years to come.

Because of his brother's notoriety, Vladimir was a marked man at the university. Radical students sought him out, and he joined a Populist group with a terrorist orientation not long after his matriculation. On December 16 he participated in a student demonstration protesting the stifling regimen imposed by the Ministry of Education. He was arrested that evening and spent two days in jail. His offense was slight, for he had not been a ringleader, but the authorities were unwilling to take chances with one who bore the subversive name Ulyanov, and he was expelled from the university along with some forty others. Ordered to leave the city, he moved to his mother's estate in the nearby village of Kokushkino. Later investigation revealed his association with the terrorist circle, and he was placed under police surveillance.

Lenin characteristically made the most of his enforced leisure. Relieved of formal course work, he devoured books with a voracious appetite and for the first time became engrossed in the literature of social protest. He was still innocent of any serious acquaintance with Marxist thought, again a rather embarrassing circumstance to Soviet hagiographers, anxious to certify his Marxist credentials at so early an age that it almost seems as if he became an orthodox Bolshevik while emerging from his mother's womb. Marxism had not yet attracted any significant portion of the Russian intelligentsia, though in faraway Switzerland a group of exiles headed by Georgi Plekhanov had founded in 1883 the first genuinely Marxist organization in the history of the Russian revolutionary movement. Agrarian Populism, ostensibly the variety of socialism espoused by Alexander Ulyanov, continued to strike the fancy of the radical youth. It was based on the belief that the peasant commune would become the nucleus of a socialist society and that the stage of industrial capitalism—the path of the bourgeois West—might be avoided altogether. But the notion that terror was not only a legitimate but an efficacious political weapon had lost much of its luster, and the doctrine had no politically significant following during the remainder of Alexander III's reign. Nikolai Chernyshevsky, author of the famous novel *What Is To Be Done?* (1863), still served as the chief intellectual inspiration for those who, if not convinced revolutionaries, were given to "dangerous thoughts" and an uneasy social conscience. Lenin had read the book at too early an age to be receptive to its message, and sophisticated critics of a later age would find its plot ludicrous, its characters wooden, and its prose execrable. But a second reading so impressed him that he began to model himself on the one memorable character in the book, Rakhmetov, a revolutionary ascetic whose life was dedicated to creating a new and better society. Lenin went on to Chernyshevsky's other works. "I read him pencil in hand and made long extracts of what I was reading," he is reported to have said in 1904. "Chernyshevsky's encyclopedic knowledge, the brilliance of his revolutionary views, and his ruthless polemical talent captivated me."[3] Insofar as Lenin's conversion to revolution can be traced to intellectual causes, this reacquaintance with the great martyr of Populist socialism seems to have been a good deal more decisive than his subsequent encounter with Karl Marx.

Lenin's respectful request for readmission to the university was refused, nor was he permitted to leave Russia to study or to "take the cure" at a European spa. But the ban on his residence in Kazan was lifted, and he returned there with the Ulyanov family in the fall of 1888. These were times of anxiety and frustration for the young man. Without a university diploma he was barred from a professional career, and no other occupational choice for one of his abilities and station in life seemed possible. No wonder his personality changed for the worse. Assured, modest, and apparently well adjusted, he became moody and taciturn, his insecurity concealed by sarcasm and a kind of arrogant cynicism. This prolonged period of uncertainty and enforced leisure was probably much more important in shaping his revolutionary psyche than the "revenge" he supposedly sought for his brother's execution, a romantic version favored by a number of Western writers.

Lenin's mother later attempted to interest him in farming—she purchased a small estate near Samara (now Kuibyshev)—but he was hardly a man of the soil, even as a gentleman farmer, and the exploitative nature of his relationship with the peasants was distasteful to him. Not surprisingly, his Soviet biographers have remained discreetly silent about this brief but significant episode in his career.

From the spring of 1889 through the summer of 1893 Lenin and his family spent the long winters in Samara and the short summers at the nearby estate. Although there were periods of bitterness, even despair, Lenin was not given to self-pity nor a prey to that typically Russian disease of "oblomovism," a kind of fatalistic lethargy described so ably in Ivan Goncharov's novel *Oblomov* (1859). He had joined a Populist circle in Kazan, and in Samara he became a member of a similar group, though details of these associations are sparse indeed. Lenin himself avoided mentioning this aspect of his revolutionary career on the premise that the pillar of Russian Marxism should not have been consorting with Populists even at this formative stage of his intellectual development. The Soviet guardians of the Lenin cult obviously agree with him.

The persistence of Lenin's mother in interceding with the authorities in St. Petersburg to allow her son to take the law examination without additional classes finally prevailed. Permission was granted in the summer of 1890. Lenin had already read a good deal of law on his own, and by strenuous cramming and extraordinary self-discipline he was able to master a four-year law course in little more than a year. He passed his examinations —one in the spring and one in the fall of 1891—with high distinction at St. Petersburg University. After further confrontation with the bureaucracy, he obtained a document attesting to his loyalty and good character and was then permitted to practice law. Andrei Khardin, an old chess opponent and a reputable lawyer in Samara of liberal political views, provided him with employment.

In his own mind Lenin had already broken with the prevailing social order, but it seems doubtful that he was emotionally prepared to burn his bridges and to abandon the workaday world for the precarious life of a full-time revolutionary. It can be argued, of course, that the concept of the *professional* revolutionary was unknown at the time, except in isolated instances, and that the idea was to become one of Lenin's chief contributions to revolutionary theory and practice. The circumstances of his conversion to Marxist socialism have been the subject of endless speculation, and the Soviet verdict naturally tends to under-play his prolonged dalliance with the Populists. He himself, with some exaggeration, dated it from the early part of 1889 when he read the first volume of Marx's *Capital* and Plekhanov's *Our Differences,* the latter a convincing argument for the Marxist position by one who had already traversed the ideological path that Lenin was just beginning. By the close of 1891 he con-sidered himself a full-fledged Marxist (at least in retrospect), yet he had by no means shed the intellectual baggage of his earlier convictions. It may be that he never did, for orthodoxy in ideo-logical matters is scarcely an exact science, and his political genius lay precisely in his ability to adapt an "alien" doctrine, designed for the industrialized, bourgeois society of Western Europe to the "backward," largely agrarian society of tsarist Rus-sia. No one is qualified to determine whether he was really an "orthodox" Marxist or not. The master himself had died in 1883, and his partner Friedrich Engels declined the role of ideological watchdog. The problem is further complicated by Marx's own comments on the Russian situation—meager though they were—that tended to support the Populist view that the peasant com-mune might indeed be the key to socialism. Nor were the Populists themselves doctrinaire sectarians: many of their theo-rists found much to admire in the Marxist legacy.

Lenin retained, for example, his "special attitude" toward terror, recognizing in theory the validity of the Marxist view that political murder was essentially self-defeating as a revolutionary weapon. But he stubbornly maintained that any means, includ-ing terror, might be a legitimate device in a particular situation if it served the sacred cause of the revolution. With a somewhat similar perversity, unrelated to the question of terror, he opposed those who would attempt to feed the starving peasants caught in the great famine of 1891–92. The death rate, including victims of cholera and typhus following in the wake of the famine, was especially high in the Samara district. Lenin complained—the quotation is probably inexact—that "all the talk about feeding the hungry is the expression of the usual sugar and honey senti-mentalism which is peculiar to our intelligentsia."[4] His argument that the social order was the basic cause and that the peasants would be driven into the cities and "proletarianized"—presum-ably to become class-conscious consumers of Marxist propaganda

—had a certain remorseless logic to it. But such reasoning was at best pseudo-Marxist, and his sentiments were apparently unique among Russian socialists, whatever their doctrinal affiliation.

Lenin took part in various discussion groups and proved a formidable debater, never the kind, then or later, who could suffer fools gladly. An earnest, one might even say presumptuous and slightly priggish young man, he won respect by his intellectual abilities but was something of a "loner" and formed no lasting friendships and acquired no disciples except the members of his family. As a matter of principle—a revolutionary must keep fit—he followed a routine of physical exercise with the same purposeful intensity that he gave to his theoretical studies. His law practice was desultory and pursued only for the sake of appearances. He defended a number of petty criminals, all of whom were patently guilty, and failed to win a single acquittal. His employer remained a model of discretion and sympathetic understanding for the duration of their unconventional partnership. Lenin's first literary effort, a lengthy review of a book on the agrarian question, was rejected for publication by *Russkaya mysl* ("Russian Thought"), a liberal journal of considerable prestige. It was a blow to his pride, but the essay, largely an ambitious summary, lacked originality and did not appear in print until 1923 when it became the first item of his *Collected Works*.

Life in the provincial backwater of Samara palled on Lenin long before he decided to leave. Probably he would have remained in St. Petersburg after completing his examinations had he been free of family obligations. But his sister Olga had died of typhoid fever in 1891, and his distraught mother needed the moral support of her eldest son. By the fall of 1893 the problem of returning to the capital—the mecca of the revolutionary intelligentsia—was eased by the decision of the other members of the family to move to Moscow, where his brother Dmitri enrolled in the university. In St. Petersburg, as in Samara, he acquired respectability by nominal employment in the law office of a liberal "patron," though his opinion of lawyers had soured: they were "professional windbags" and "born bearers of the ideas of bourgeois society."[5]

Ample self-assurance and reliable references (as well as his family name) did not automatically admit Lenin into the conspiratorial circles of the local revolutionaries. Outsiders were always suspect, for police infiltration was routinely practiced, although the authorities considered the arid theorizing of the Marxists less dangerous than the bomb throwers and other assassins who lurked in the ranks of the Populists. At length, most likely in the spring of 1894, he became a member of a small group of socialists headed by Stepan Radchenko, a student at the Technological Institute. They had only minimal contact with the city's large working class, in whose name the Marxists were the self-appointed spokesmen. Not long after his formal admission to the Radchenko circle Lenin met his future wife, Nadezhda Krupskaya, a grave young girl with a petite face and snub nose who taught evening and Sunday classes to illiterate workers. She later recalled his scornful laugh when someone spoke of the importance of the Illiteracy Committee. "Well, if anyone wants to save the country by working in the Illiteracy Committee," he said sarcastically, "let him go ahead."[6] The founder of what came to be called Bolshevism was too impatient to get on with the struggle against Tsarism to waste his time on humanitarian or educational projects, however well intentioned. Despite his initial disdain he was ultimately drawn into the committee's activity, for cultural philanthropy furnished a veneer of respectability for more active revolutionary work.

Lenin's intellectual growth was rapid, and his physical maturity seemed to outstrip his chronological age. Still a young man—he was twenty-four in the spring of 1894—he had already become quite bald, and his serious mien, together with a mustache and beard, made him look a good ten years older. He was nicknamed "Baldy" by the workers in his instructional circle, who used to say that "from all his knowledge he had lost his hair," and to his colleagues, mostly of the same age group, he became simply the "old man."

By the latter part of 1894 Lenin had acquired a local reputation as a Marxist theoretician, although his view of capitalism was still somewhat primitive. He equated it with "reaction" without a sophisticated understanding of its complexity or its dynamic role in European society. As for revolutionary strategy, he retained much of the Populist heritage of direct action while rejecting the notion of parliamentary democracy that Western

socialists found quite compatible with the class struggle and other
tenets of formal Marxism.

Lenin's literary ambitions had been frustrated thus far. But in
1895 he published his first work (other than a hectographed
essay of limited circulation), the product of an intellectual encounter with Peter Struve, a gifted young scholar who was to
acquire the invidious distinction of being Russia's first "Legal
Marxist." Struve's *Critical Remarks on the Question of Russia's
Economic Development* (1894) had unexpectedly passed the
censor and made him an overnight intellectual celebrity. The
term "Legal Marxism" was not coined until the turn of the
century and became one of opprobrium, at least in Lenin's entourage, but it was certainly unfair that works couched in Aesopian language to evade the censorship should be said to have
strayed upon the forbidden ground of doctrinal heresy. Marxism
became something of a fad among the liberal intelligentsia not
otherwise attracted to the revolutionary struggle. Ponderous
tomes with soporific titles—pamphleteering was taboo—appeared
in increasing numbers to satisfy the unexpected market. The
subversive propaganda, if indeed any could be found, was invariably concealed behind statistical data and dreary abstractions
seeking to demonstrate that industrial capitalism represented
"progress" as opposed to the "feudal" agrarian society that the
Populists found so praiseworthy. Any hint of direct action against
the autocracy was bound to attract the literal-minded censors,
who could recognize inflammatory prose but were out of their
depth when it came to economic theory and scholastic disputa-
tion.

Lenin too became an eager practitioner of Legal Marxism,
though he denounced the adulteration of the revolutionary message that others, presumably less discriminating than he, were
tempted to perpetrate. He wrote an extensive review of Struve's
book, and later the two met frequently to discuss their differing
interpretations of Russian capitalism. A mutual acquaintance and
fellow Marxist, Alexander Potresov, invited Lenin to submit
his review as part of a symposium he was planning on Russian
social democracy. A lengthier and less polemical version was
printed in the spring of 1895 together with essays contributed by
Struve, Plekhanov, and others. Entitled *The Economic Content*

of Populism and Its Critique in Mr. Struve's Book and signed
with the pen name K. Tulin, it was written in a critical but not
unfriendly vein, stamping its author as a self-proclaimed "orthodox" Marxist who hoped, by gentle admonition, to lead his
errant colleague back to the truth faith. Unfortunately for his
budding literary career, the collaborative work was held up by
the censors, who objected particularly to the seditious tone of
Lenin's article. Almost a year later the police seized and burned
the entire edition with the exception of a hundred copies or so
that were "liberated" from the printing plant.

Lenin had been troubled by poor health in the early months
of 1895. Stomach upsets, very likely brought on by overwork and
nervous tension, were followed by a severe attack of pneumonia.
His mother and his sister Anna came from Moscow to minister
to him. In the spring he received permission to go abroad for
medical treatment, although his chief mission was to establish
contact with the Marxist émigrés in Switzerland. First and foremost among them was Plekhanov, already an infallible oracle
to his eager disciples in Russia. Brilliant and erudite, a "Westernized" Russian with catholic tastes and wide-ranging intellectual
interests, he lacked any genuine "feel" for practical politics and
was one day to be embalmed, figuratively speaking, with the
historian's cliché: the "Father of Russian Marxism." Neither
Lenin nor Plekhanov furnished an account of their first meeting,
which took place in Geneva, but the latter was impressed by his
visitor, who accepted as a matter of course the humble role of
pupil in relation to the master. Lenin went on to Zurich, where
he called on Paul Axelrod, another revered figure among the
Swiss expatriates whose prestige was second only to Plekhanov's.
Axelrod found him to be a "modest, businesslike, serious young
man, without the slightest vanity." He read with interest the
"Tulin" essay that Lenin brought him, finding it flawed from a
literary standpoint but revealing the "temperament of a fighting
flame, a feeling that for the author Marxism was not an abstract
doctrine but a weapon of revolutionary struggle." The next day,
informed that Lenin and "Tulin" were the same, he ventured to
disagree with his young compatriot's contemptuous attitude toward the liberal bourgeoisie. Since all elements of Russian society faced the same task in overthrowing the tsarist autocracy,

why not work together in a temporary political alliance? Lenin—he was, of course, still Ulyanov to his host—smiled and observed that Plekhanov had made the same point, putting it in a different way: "You turn your back to the liberals and we our faces."[7] After a discussion that continued for several days, he professed himself convinced of the essential correctness of his mentors' view. Indeed, he did moderate his strictures on the liberals upon his return to Russia. But the argument was fundamental to revolutionary strategy, and his temporary deference to the wisdom of his superiors did not alter his visceral reaction that Russian liberalism was decadent and undependable.

A dutiful son, Lenin wrote regularly to his mother during his four-month trip but cautiously confined his letters to personal trivia. He stayed for a time at a Swiss health resort for his "tiresome stomach trouble" and, like most European travelers, found that his expenses exceeded his budget. His requests and hints for more funds—"my money goes the devil knows where"—were presumably honored, for Maria Ulyanova took great pride in her son's accomplishments and invariably strained her modest resources to provide for his financial needs. His labored German proved inadequate for conversation, but his French, like that of a good many educated Russians, was passable. In Berlin he met Karl Kautsky, perhaps the most famous Marxist theoretician aside from Engels himself (who died in London shortly afterward). In Paris, which made a "very pleasant impression," he became acquainted with the socialist leader Paul Lafargue, Marx's son-in-law, who expressed polite skepticism—and rightly so—of Lenin's claim that the Russian workers were enthusiastic about Marxism.

The Okhrana was fully aware of Lenin's presence abroad and that medical treatment was only an incidental purpose of his journey. He returned to Russia in September, 1895, and the border police singled out his luggage for a special search but failed to discover the illegal literature hidden in the false bottom of his suitcase. After contacting Marxist sympathizers in Vilna and Moscow, and presumably after a reunion with his family, he settled down again in St. Petersburg. The comparative anonymity of his former stay was now replaced by police surveillance. He nevertheless took a more active part in the writing and distribution of propaganda leaflets in working-class districts, using the aliases Fyodor and Nikolai Petrovich. One of his friends and associates was Julius Martov, a young intellectual of Jewish origin for whom Lenin in later years retained personal affection despite their subsequent political quarrel. ("I am sorry, deeply sorry, that Martov is not with us," Lenin would one day remark after his elevation to political power. "What a splendid comrade he was, what an absolutely sincere man!") [8]

Martov was instrumental in convincing Lenin and his associates that "agitation" among the workers was preferable to the sterile tactics of "propaganda." Political indoctrination, in other words, should be replaced by appeals concentrating upon immediate economic issues. If strikes could then be incited, the workers would learn through practical experience, since the government would inevitably side with the employers, that politics was not simply arid theorizing by intellectuals.

Lenin also demonstrated his flexibility by abandoning his former hostility to constitutional democracy. The reasons for his conversion to Western-style socialism are not easy to fathom—the influence of Plekhanov, Axelrod, and Struve may have been decisive—but his first clear statement came in an obituary of Engels written for a Geneva publication in which he maintained that the "most immediate and important task of the Russian socialists" was the "winning of political freedom."[9] He now admitted, though not in so many words, that he had overestimated the development of Russian capitalism and that the major adversary was not the bourgeoisie but the tsarist autocracy itself.

The various Marxist groups in St. Petersburg had finally achieved unity in the fall of 1895, and in late December they adopted an unduly pretentious name—Union of Struggle for the Emancipation of the Working Class. Soviet accounts portray Lenin as the founder and leader of the group but remain uniformly reticent about substantiating their claim with documentary evidence. On the night of December 20, a week before the Union acquired its formal designation, some forty members, Lenin among them, were arrested. Within a month most of the remaining leaders were also in custody. A police agent within their ranks, a dentist by the name of Mikhailov, was apparently responsible for almost wiping out the promising socialist movement in the capital. Many labor leaders were disgruntled if not embittered by what they regarded as faulty tactics on the part of their "revolutionary comrades"—the intellectuals. "They took to scattering proclamations all over," complained one, "and in two months destroyed the work of years."[10]

Tsarist prisons were not designed for the comfort of their inmates. Yet the conditions of incarceration, while markedly varied, were comparatively lax, reflecting the complacent inefficiency that characterized the bureaucratic structure of the old regime. "Politicals" constituted an elite group for whom special privileges, such as ample reading material from the outside, were readily available. And for those with money almost anything within reason could be obtained. The prison in St. Petersburg was well endowed with a good library and other amenities lacking in more provincial institutions, and Lenin's confinement became in some respects an enforced sabbatical in which he had the leisure to pursue his theoretical studies. The spartan habits he had acquired as a boy proved useful in combating melancholia and other psychic disorders common to prison life. He maintained a regular schedule of calisthenics, language study, reading, and research. His stomach condition actually improved, due no doubt to the relaxing solitude of his daily routine. Other than the proper maintenance of his cell, no assigned tasks were required of him. He supplemented the drab prison fare with food and drink from the canteen or outside sources, and his mother and sister, who visited regularly, supplied him with books and money and served as couriers for messages to associates both in Russia and abroad.

The technique of secret correspondence had already been well developed among imprisoned revolutionaries. Books, ordinarily given only a superficial inspection, served as the chief medium of communication. Milk and occasionally lemon juice were used to form tiny dots in the middle of printed letters, and the message could be decoded by heating the page. Lenin made inkwells out of bread, and when necessity arose they could be easily swallowed. "Today I have eaten six inkpots," he joked in one of his secret missives.

"I have everything I need and even more than I need," Lenin wrote his sister Anna on January 24, 1896. "I sleep about nine hours a day and dream about the various chapters in my next book."[11] The book, begun in prison and completed during his

Siberian exile, was eventually published as *The Development of Capitalism in Russia*. Lenin's sentence, banishment for three years under police surveillance, came after fourteen months of imprisonment, and he was so absorbed with his research that he received the news with some regret. "If I had been in prison a while longer," he told his brother Dmitri, "I could have finished the book."[12]

Granted a three-day "furlough" before leaving on his long journey, Lenin had a reunion with a number of his comrades, some of them also preparing for exile in Siberia. He was given the additional privilege of traveling via Moscow, where he saw his family, and then set out at his own expense on the Trans-Siberian Railroad. Those with money and influence were spared the inconvenience and humiliation of an armed escort and stop-overs in local jails. Lenin wrote several letters to his mother en route and reported that he was "far less exhausted" than he expected despite the "devilish slowness" of the train. His emotional state had not been of the best before his departure, and he reassured her that he felt quite calm: "I have left my nerves in Moscow. The reason for nerves was the uncertainty of the position and nothing else. But now that there is less uncertainty, I feel well." At Krasnoyarsk on the Yenisei River he interrupted his journey for further word on his final place of exile. A well-connected friend had put him in touch with a local official (a Populist sympathizer as it turned out) who was apparently able to assign him to the region south of Krasnoyarsk, where the climate, if scarcely benign, was less frigid than the more northerly latitudes. The agreeable official also introduced him to Claudia Popova, a wealthy patroness of revolutionaries, and she furnished him (and other exiles in transit) free room and board in her spacious and comfortable residence. He remained about two months waiting for the spring thaw to clear the ice from the river, for the trip south had to be made by steamboat. Most of his days were spent studying in the splendid library assembled by a rich merchant and bibliophile, Gennadi Yudin. In 1906 most of this famous collection was sold to the Library of Congress in Washington.

On May 18 Lenin reached Minusinsk, the steamboat terminus, and then set out in a horse-drawn cart, escorted by two gendarmes, for his final destination, the village of Shushenskoye. He rented a room in a substantial wooden cottage and soon settled into his familiar routine of study and research. His monthly government allowance of eight rubles (about four dollars at the rate of exchange then prevailing) was parsimonious but sufficient for basic necessities, and his mother sent him additional money as well as parcels of books, clothing, and other items. His sister Anna usually received the most burdensome requests—those relating to his scholarly interests. She seems to have done her best as a kind of long-distance secretary, research assistant, and literary agent, but her impatient brother nevertheless scolded her at times for delays and minor lapses. Her memoirs, though wholly orthodox Leniniana, offer a few hints at the resentment she must have felt upon occasion.

For Lenin it was a lonely life, but there were diversions: chess, swimming, hunting, and ice-skating, depending on the weather and the season of the year. The postal service was slow and deliveries infrequent—usually twice a week—but far better than the less accessible regions of Siberia. Lenin maintained a voluminous correspondence with friends, relatives, and fellow exiles. It was his chief link with the outside world. "Today" (March 8, 1898), he wrote his mother, "I received a pile of letters from all parts of Russia and Siberia and have therefore been in a holiday mood all day."[13]

In the spring of 1898 the monotony was broken by the arrival of Nadezhda Krupskaya and her mother. She had been arrested in the summer of 1896 and sentenced to three years' exile in Ufa, a city in the southern Urals. Her petition to join Lenin as his "fiancée" was granted on condition that they marry at once, for the "companionship" favored by the emancipated young revolutionaries was impermissible to the strait-laced authorities. But it was over two months before the necessary formalities could be arranged and their union solemnized in a church ceremony (civil marriages were illegal), a technicality that has distressed more than one Soviet biographer. It was a good match, at least temperamentally and ideologically, but something of a puzzle as far as intimate—especially libidinous—details are concerned. The available printed sources are uninformative, and others (if they exist) have been kept under tight security in Soviet archives. The personal lives of government leaders are regarded as strictly private, even posthumously, and for so awesome a figure as Lenin speculation about his sex life or the state of his mental health is regarded as bad taste bordering on sacrilege and therefore unpublishable.

Even as a young woman Krupskaya (she was invariably referred to by her surname) lacked "sex appeal," and in middle age, judging from photographs, she became, if not shapeless, decidedly unattractive. They were to remain childless, though apparently not by choice, leading to the tentative conclusion that one or both was sterile. A less likely possibility, that impotence, frigidity, or a low sex drive was involved, is suggested only by the curiously pragmatic nature of their marriage—more like a business partnership than a romantic attachment. But Lenin unquestionably had deep affection for her, and Krupskaya, whose didactic "memoirs" have all the spontaneity of a government document, felt obliged to leaven her narrative with asides indicating that their life was happy and not altogether a political union.

The honeymooners worked on a translation of the first volume of Sidney and Beatrice Webb's Industrial Democracy, a well-paid assignment procured by Peter Struve, who corresponded somewhat irregularly but performed valuable literary chores for Lenin. Krupskaya later copied several drafts of The Development of Capitalism in Russia (the title was suggested by Struve), and the manuscript was legally published the following spring in St. Petersburg under the pseudonym Vladimir Ilyn. A formidable work of some six hundred pages, replete with statistical tables and copious footnotes, it established his reputation not only as a Marxist scholar but as a serious economist as well. He tended to overstate his case by "proving" on the basis of insufficient data that capitalism had made greater inroads upon Russian agriculture than subsequent investigation has shown. But he demonstrated easily enough that the Populists—slipshod and naive economists at best—were mistaken in believing that the old village economy could be the springboard to socialism.

As the second winter of exile approached, Lenin had moments of nostalgia but never openly admitted it. In a letter to his sister Maria, who had gone to study in Brussels, he expressed envy at her location. "During the first period of my exile I decided not to look at a map of European Russia or Europe; there was always such a bitter taste in my mouth when I opened those maps and looked at the various black dots on them." Meanwhile he had learned to be patient: "I looked mostly backward, I suppose, but now I am looking ahead."[14] Inevitably, despite his calm resignation, he felt that events were passing him by. One, of little contemporary importance, but of subsequent notoriety, was the so-called First Congress of the Russian Social Democratic Labor Party held secretly in Minsk (March 13–15, 1898). This obscure meeting was the unlikely birthplace of the Communist Party of the Soviet Union. The police claimed to have arrested eight of the nine delegates in less than a year, and virtually all that emerged from the gathering was an agreement that Struve (who was not present) should prepare a "manifesto." An unexceptional document, it did contain one memorable passage: "The further east one goes in Europe, the weaker, more cowardly, and more abject the bourgeoisie becomes politically, and the more its cultural and political tasks fall upon the proletariat." The sentiment is recognizably Leninist, although Struve, paradoxically, was to abandon Marxism within a few years and ended his career as a "liberal on the Right."

Rather more significant in the history of Marxism, including its Russian variant, was the appearance of a series of articles by Eduard Bernstein, a young German Social Democrat. Later reworked as a book and published in 1899 (the English title was *Evolutionary Socialism*), it scandalized orthodox Marxists and produced an unbridled flow of vituperation and rebuttal. "Revisionism" was thus born, and its proponents argued persuasively that far from being "renegades" and "traitors," they were simply trying to preserve the viable essence of Marxism. Blind adherence to the letter of sacred texts would lead to nothing but obsolete and irrelevant dogma, whereas appropriate modifications in the light of actual economic change could only redeem and strengthen the cause of socialism. Why not jettison the pseudo-science of "surplus value" and "dialectical materialism," the false gods of the "class struggle" and the "increasing misery of the proletariat"? Such doctrines no longer served any useful purpose, for it had become self-evident that workers, like everyone else, were enjoying higher rather than lower incomes and that the goals of socialism could be reached without violence and bloodshed.

Most of what Bernstein and his supporters said was eminently reasonable. After all, they were merely providing a conscious rationale for a de facto process of "bourgeoisification" that—unintentionally and largely unnoticed—had been underway for many years in the socialist parties of the West. None of the Revisionists had consciously "betrayed" Marx. Even their vehement critics, while intellectually committed to the master's most apocalyptic visions, had gradually lost their revolutionary zeal. The overwhelming majority of the Russian Marxists were unaware of the forces that had undermined the militancy of the venerable European parties and were appalled at Bernstein's heresy. Lenin waited for a copy of the pernicious book with growing impatience. He and Krupskaya devoured it when at last the notorious volume arrived. "We have already read more than half," he wrote his mother on September 1, 1899, "and its contents astonish us more and more as we go on. It is incredibly weak theoretically. . . . In effect it is opportunism . . . and *cowardly* opportunism at that. . . . There is little doubt that it will be a fiasco. Bernstein's statement that many Russians agree with him . . . made us very indignant."[15] Plekhanov and Axelrod were equally aghast, and the former, who declared that he "almost took sick from these articles," denounced Bernstein so abusively that Kautsky, who edited the leading organ of German Social Democracy, omitted several passages when he published Plekhanov's rejoinder.

The Russian mutation of the Revisionist argument—Bernstein himself was not involved—was labeled "Economism." According to the oversimplified view of its enemies, Economism stressed the immediate bread-and-butter grievances of the workers over the long-range tasks of political revolution. Katherine Kuskova, the wife of the Marxist economist Sergei Prokopovich, unwittingly gave it currency when a speech she made at a meeting in St. Petersburg was summarized and distributed without her knowledge. A copy of this "Credo," as it came to be known, reached Lenin in Siberia, and he wrote a stinging and devastating reply. Unsatisfied, he mobilized the nearby exiles of Marxist persuasion —seventeen in all—and held a conference in September, 1899. All of them duly signed his "Protest of the Russian Social Democrats," and additional signatures were obtained when copies were circulated in other parts of Siberia. One of the Russian socialist journals abroad, nominally associated with Economist views, published the "Protest" without delay, noting in an editorial comment that the "Credo" represented "muddled thinking" without much support in the movement as a whole. But Lenin had skillfully inflated the issue and was to make even greater political mileage in the future by exposing the alleged fallacies of Economism.

As the end of his three-year sentence approached, Lenin grew restless and impatient. He slept poorly, "grew terribly thin," and made elaborate plans for a new Social Democratic party that would at last unite all Russian Marxists in a single organization. A newspaper, to be published abroad, would furnish ideological guidance for the party faithful. On one occasion the police searched the cottage but gave up before discovering his illegal correspondence, which lay carelessly on the bottom shelf of the bookcase. The incident did not furnish a pretext for adding to his term—not an unusual occurrence—and on February 10, 1900, he set out with Krupskaya and her mother for European Russia. They traveled by sled to Achinsk and then by rail to Ufa. There Krupskaya was to complete her term of exile, while her husband, forbidden to settle in metropolitan centers or university towns, chose Pskov for its proximity to the capital and to the Russian border. Politics, as always, took precedence over domestic bliss in the Ulyanov household. Lenin slipped off illegally to Moscow for a family visit, and went on to St. Petersburg, where he met Vera Zasulich, a colleague of Plekhanov and Axelrod who had just arrived from Western Europe. He reached Pskov precisely a month after leaving Shushenskoye.

Lenin acquired a respectable "cover" and a means of livelihood by working in the provincial statistical office. But judging from his busy pace—conspiratorial meetings and numerous trips to other cities—his superiors must have been as indulgent as his previous employers. In May he received permission for a trip to Germany but delayed his departure in order to acquire more contacts and to arrange financial support for the projected newspaper and a new theoretical journal. Early in June, while he was illegally in St. Petersburg, the police picked him up (along with his friend Martov) and detained him for ten days. They discovered 1,400 rubles sewn into the lining of his suit but not a list of contacts written in invisible ink on an ordinary invoice. For some unexplained reason—certainly not lack of evidence or knowledge of his activities—he was released and escorted to Polotsk near Moscow, where he had received permission to visit his mother. A police official there confiscated his passport, but Lenin, the hereditary nobleman, had a way with the lesser breed of civil servants and threatened an appeal to higher authority. The cowed official respectfully returned the precious document. After a visit of several weeks with his wife in Ufa—the journey was prolonged by politically motivated stopovers going and coming—Lenin left Pskov for Switzerland on July 29. Well beyond the stage of revolutionary apprenticeship, he went abroad this time with justifiable confidence in his reputation and ability, no longer the lowly disciple of five years before.

CHAPTER III

The Forging of a Bolshevik

LENIN FOUND THE ÉMIGRÉ SOCIAL DEMOCRATIC MOVEMENT IN serious disarray. Plekhanov and the other "elder statesmen" were at odds with most of the younger Marxists, some of whom sided with the Economists and sympathized with Bernstein on the Revisionist question. Despite his past fulminations against heresy, Lenin conceived his role as that of unifier and conciliator. His newspaper, to be named *Iskra* ("The Spark") in reference to Pushkin's phrase about the unsuccessful Decembrist Revolt of 1825—"From the spark shall grow the flame"—was to be the organ of the whole Russian party. Revisionists, Economists, and even non-Marxists might contribute on the understanding that their views would be criticized by the editors. As Lenin put it in his "prospectus"—a draft statement of the editorial board—"We not only do not reject polemics between comrades in our organs, but, on the contrary, we are ready to give them a great deal of space."[1] Financial problems were anticipated and no potential sources of revenue could be offended.

Unfortunately, Lenin's arrival in Geneva was poorly timed. Plekhanov, recently engaged in a bitter struggle against the Revisionists, was in a highly irritable and emotional state of mind. Even his normal behavior was apt to be prickly and his manner somewhat aloof, except among intimates, and he frequently conveyed the impression, perhaps unintentionally, of intellectual arrogance and condescension toward inferiors. Now he was being asked to lend his prestige to an enterprise that would allow his enemies access to what he had assumed would be an orthodox Social Democratic publication. He reacted with righteous indignation to what he could only regard as intellectual chicanery. Lenin, who still considered himself a staunch "Plekhanovite," was taken aback by the "suspicious, distrustful" attitude of his former mentor. As he wrote in a confidential memorandum first published in 1924 ("How the 'Spark' Was Nearly Extinguished"), "I tried to observe caution, avoiding all 'sore' points, but the constant restraint that I had to place on myself could not but greatly affect my mood." Plekhanov railed against his émigré opponents as "swindlers and rogues" and "displayed complete intolerance, an inability or an unwillingness to understand opposing arguments, and, to be precise, insincerity." He also objected to Lenin's proposed editorial statement for *Iskra:* it was written in an "opportunist" spirit and needed more literary elegance and an "elevated" tone (Lenin's style, though always serviceable, was apt to be plodding). In later conferences, which included Axelrod, Zasulich, and Potresov, Plekhanov maintained for the most part a petulant silence, occasionally throwing in a venomous remark, and finally agreed to a six-man editorial board that would give him two votes. It was in this unpleasant "atmosphere of ultimatums" that *Iskra* was born.

The episode left a lasting impression on Lenin. "My 'infatuation' with Plekhanov disappeared as if by magic," he wrote, "and I felt offended and embittered to an unbelievable degree. Never, never in my life, had I regarded any other man with such sincere respect and veneration, never had I stood before any man so 'humbly'—and never before had I been so brutally 'kicked.' "[2] This emotionally charged passage was written soon after their quarrel, and as time and geographical separation mellowed both men Lenin's "infatuation" returned in some degree. He recognized Plekhanov's faults, and never again was he naive enough to assume that admirable ideas were necessarily associated with admirable men. He acknowledged, at least implicitly, that Plekhanov's outbursts against "renegades" concealed sound judgment about the proper course of Russian Social Democracy. Eventually he was to become so "orthodox" that even his old teacher could not meet his rigid standards. For his part, Plekhanov forgave his impetuous young colleague and soon came to respect Lenin's organizational ability and editorial talent. "That Petrov [Lenin] is a good fellow I never doubted," he wrote Axelrod early in 1901. "It's too bad that purely administrative work prevents him from much reading and writing. However, the second number of *Iskra* is nonetheless *very good.* I am reading it with great satisfaction."[3]

Perhaps the chief contribution to their businesslike relationship lay in the physical removal of *Iskra* as a publishing enterprise to Germany, where the Social Democratic Party furnished support on such technical matters as printing and distribution. Plekhanov's intractability had won only a Pyrrhic victory. As Zasulich had remarked to Lenin, Plekhanov "is like a greyhound: he will shake you and shake you and will let you go; you are like a bulldog: you have a deadly grip."[4] Lenin became the de facto managing editor, while the two most important members of the editorial board representing the "old guard"— Plekhanov in Geneva and Axelrod in Zurich—were consulted largely by mail. The tacit arrangement allowed Plekhanov a free hand with *Zarya* ("The Dawn"), a high-level intellectual journal designed to complement *Iskra's* more plebeian appeal.

Lenin resided in Munich, the newspaper was initially printed in Leipzig (the first issue appeared in the new year but was dated December, 1900), and the distribution center was Berlin. Returning travelers and professional smugglers carried the contraband across the frontier, while a network of agents distributed the paper inside Russia. The job was dangerous and, except for a sense of revolutionary accomplishment, unrewarding. Little or no financial gain could be expected, nor did these obscure foot soldiers of Social Democracy share in the prestige that accrued to the party's general staff, living abroad in safety. The high rate of attrition was partly but not solely due to the vigilance of the secret police. The Okhrana maintained a network of agents and informers in the larger European cities, and it was fully aware of Lenin's identity (despite his various aliases) and his role in the publication of *Iskra.*

Lenin's first winter away from his homeland was emotionally depressing. His editorial duties were demanding, but he confessed in a letter to his mother that he felt "rather lonely" and that his way of life was "rather purposeless." "I keep hoping to arrange my affairs more systematically," he reported, "but I don't seem to manage it. Things will surely go better in the spring, and I shall get 'on the rails.' " "Things" did go better in the spring, largely because Krupskaya completed her term of exile in Ufa and joined him in Munich. She freed him from many of the petty chores of daily existence and assumed the post of secretary to *Iskra's* editorial board. The newspaper, planned as

a biweekly, became virtually a monthly because of various publication difficulties, principally the burden of editorial and administrative work that had fallen on Lenin. Its impact on the
Russian worker was negligible, for Lenin concentrated on brow-
beating the Economists and other recondite issues quite remote
from the political understanding of the urban masses. But it did
influence some of the young intellectuals, and by a kind of ideological osmosis Marxism began to infiltrate the ranks of the
"advanced" workers in the larger cities. The "trade union" socialism that was sapping the vitals of revolutionary Marxism in
Western Europe made little headway in Russia even when it
became legally possible to organize workers and conduct strikes.
Nor did middle-class liberalism, with its faith in parliamentary
democracy and the beneficence of industrial capitalism, make
significant gains beyond the thin ranks of those whose education
and occupation predisposed them toward an "alien" ideology
imported from the West.

Lenin turned out a steady stream of articles for *Iskra,* and
the first issue carried an expression of his views ("Urgent Tasks
of Our Movement") that anticipated the doctrines of Bolshevism.
He still maintained that the goal of Social Democracy was the
overthrow of the autocracy and the achievement of political
liberty, but as a practical matter the working class, without
proper guidance, "inevitably becomes bourgeois." A true socialist
party "must train people who will devote the whole of their lives
to the revolution, not only their free evenings."[5] Although screen-
ing his thoughts with a good deal of rhetoric, Lenin nevertheless
became the first Marxist of consequence to deny the accepted
dogma that the proletariat, because of its class position within
capitalist society, must inevitably turn to socialism. Only the
revolutionary elite, he strongly implied, could prevent the bourgeoisification of the workers, a process already well under way
in Western Europe. From this conclusion it was only another
step to reject collaboration with the liberal bourgeoisie, and
the logical third step came with the repudiation of formal
democracy altogether. But this last proposition was never openly
acknowledged until his party gained power, and as late as 1905
he defended in print the concept of political democracy.

The famous pseudonym "N. Lenin" appeared for the first
time in a signed essay on the agrarian question, part of which

Zarya printed in December, 1901. The origin of the name is uncertain, for he never recorded the circumstances of its selection. But Plekhanov used the pen name "Volgin" in reference to the Volga River, and it seems likely that "Lenin" was a similar variation of the mighty Lena River in Siberia. The name once adopted, he seldom used any other for his signed writings.

Lenin's most important work of the "*Iskra* period" was written during the fall and winter of 1901–1902 and published in Stuttgart the following spring. Entitled *What Is to Be Done?* in tribute to Chernyshevsky's novel, it foreshadowed the organizational tactics that were to become Lenin's distinctive contribution as a Marxist and the founder of Bolshevism. For all the political and intellectual convulsions of the revolutionary movement, Russia did not yet have a Social Democratic party. Lenin aimed at a set of guidelines that would launch such a party on the "correct" path. He elaborated his cryptic remarks of the previous year, now frankly scornful of the notion that the workers, on their own initiative and because of their exploited position, would spontaneously develop a revolutionary psychology. "The history of all countries demonstrates that the working class, exclusively by its own effort, is able to develop only trade-union consciousness," he argued. Marx and Engels were themselves representatives of the "bourgeois intelligentsia," and in Russia the "theoretical doctrine of social-democracy arose altogether independently of . . . the working class movement." He concluded that the revolutionary struggle should be carried on by an elite vanguard, acting in the interest of the proletariat—that is, professionals who would dedicate their lives to the cause. The party should be centralized and its leaders well disciplined: democracy in such an organization, "amid the darkness of the autocracy and the domination of the gendarmerie, is nothing more than a *useless and harmful toy.*"

Lenin's ambivalence toward intellectuals, implicit in *What Is to Be Done?*, persisted throughout his career. On the one hand they were the indispensable leaders of the revolution; on the other, he found them to be vacillating, equivocal, and prone to "petty bourgeois opportunism." He was to discover repeatedly that unwavering "Leninists"—obviously the ideal revolutionary type—were invariably in short supply. He had now provided a formula for the party, however unorthodox it appeared to those who had studied the Marxist canon with as much care and respect as he, and it quickly established him as a brilliant theoretician in a manner that his one scholarly work and his polemical journalism had failed to do.

In April, 1902, shortly after the publication of his book, Lenin shifted his residence from Munich to London. The German police, in cooperation with the Okhrana, had evinced too great an interest in the *Iskra* venture, and it seemed advisable to seek a new base of operations. Geneva, the logical choice, Lenin deemed unsuitable because of Plekhanov's baleful presence, and he persuaded a majority of the editorial board that England provided a financially cheaper and politically freer environment than the Continent. Lenin and his wife, using the name Richter, rented a small apartment near the British Museum, and there he spent a good part of his day, like Marx before him, amid the scholarly treasures of its magnificent library. He would certainly have agreed with the master that it represented the "ideal strategic vantage point for the student of bourgeois society": the island kingdom was the citadel of world capitalism, with London its financial and commercial center, and the library custodians were seemingly unaware of the subversive uses to which their superb collection might be put. His humble quarters again served as the editorial office of *Iskra,* while printing facilities were furnished by the British Social Democratic Federation.

Lenin remained in but not *of* London. Although not precisely an austere and cloistered intellectual—as Marx had been for over thirty years—he met few Englishmen and formed no lasting attachments, either to individuals or to the customs and institutions of his temporary habitat. But he enjoyed the diversity and vitality of the vast metropolis, and the ever present extremes of degrading poverty and ostentatious wealth confirmed his diagnosis that capitalist society was decadent and doomed to perish. "Two nations!" he would mutter in English through clenched teeth.[6] Leon Trotsky, then a young and unknown revolutionary who had just escaped from Siberian exile, recalled that Lenin escorted him on a walking tour of London and remarked (the wording is inexact), "This is their famous Westminster." "Their" referred not to the British but to the ruling class.[7] Lenin's identification with the downtrodden victims of capitalism was no mere intellectual pose, for his emotional empathy was genuine enough. Yet the proletariat became almost invariably a Marxist abstraction, an idealized class bearing the embryo of a new society and serving the inscrutable purposes of history. As individuals in the flesh they seemed made of less noble stuff, and there is no indication that Lenin went out of his way, at least while abroad, to cultivate the acquaintance of particular workers and to gain insight into their feelings and aspirations. Although his manner was easy and informal with intimates, his temperament and background apparently did not permit over-familiarity with strangers, whatever their social class. He was not, after all, a social worker or psychologist, and he might well argue that as the general does not hobnob with the troops except for ceremonial appearances to boost morale, so the top-level professional revolutionary can best serve the cause in an ideological and organizational capacity.

Despite experience with English gained in translating the Webbs' book, Lenin and Krupskaya discovered that their ability to communicate orally was virtually nil. They attended all kinds of meetings simply to listen to spoken English—the soap-box orators in Hyde Park were special favorites. Later on, through an advertisement, they made arrangements for private tutoring, exchanging Russian for English lessons, and acquired reasonable facility though never mastery of the language. Their tutors and the landlady's working-class family provided ample opportunity, Krupskaya records with a kind of priggish hauteur, to study "all the abysmal philistinism of petty-bourgeois English life." Nor did the "ill-clad lumpen proletarians with pasty faces [who] hung around the pubs" escape their keen scrutiny. Where, then, was the genuine article—workers unsullied by bourgeois attitudes or the depravity of slum life? One is tempted to question the existence, in any large numbers, of such paragons of Marxian virtue, but Krupskaya insists that the "socialist" churches—of all places —abounded with "rank-and-file workers from the bench" who participated in the debates that usually followed services (their religiosity was apparently forgiven or considered only perfunctory). Lenin attended many such meetings and would supposedly comment joyfully (in agitprop clichés that one doubts were ever uttered): "They are just bursting with socialism! If a speaker starts talking rot a worker gets up right away and takes the bull by the horns, shows up the very essence of capitalism." But he was to make the painful discovery in later years that there were never enough of these militant proletarians, either in England or elsewhere in Western Europe, to promote a socialist revolution. Of course it was not their fault: invariably they were betrayed by opportunistic and treacherous leaders.

Another rift with Plekhanov, fortunately less serious than their previous encounter, frayed Lenin's nerves despite the physical distance between them. The patriarch of Russian socialism had been urged to write a platform for a future congress that would, unlike the abortive meeting in 1898, succeed in founding a uni- fied Social Democratic party. He was greatly offended when two successive drafts were severely criticized, particularly by Lenin (who produced one of his own), and to ward off a fresh schism on the editorial board a "neutral" committee drew up a com- promise document. The crisis seemed safely passed, but Ple- khanov's ego had been bruised, and he subjected one of Lenin's minor pieces—a comment on the agrarian section of the party program—to a meticulous and patronizing analysis, including a good many trivial points of style. The exasperated Lenin fired off an angry retort (May 14, 1902): "You have fine ideas of tact toward editorial colleagues! . . . If you have sought to make our common work impossible, you can very quickly attain this aim by the road you have chosen. Regarding personal and not business relations, you have already definitely spoiled them or, rather, you have succeeded in breaking them off completely."[8]

Axelrod and Zasulich interceded in the dispute and finally persuaded Plekhanov to make a conciliatory gesture—not exactly an apology but about as close to an act of contrition as the haughty patrician could be brought to make. "You have taken offense unjustly," he wrote. "I had no desire to insult you . . . I will do anything I can so as not to irritate a comrade who is so useful to the cause and who, believe this, I respect with all my heart."[9] Lenin responded generously, apparently sensing the effort it must have taken him to write in such a vein: "A great weight fell from my shoulders when I received your letter, which put an end to thoughts of 'civil war.'" After further mollifying words and a discussion of business affairs, he added a revealing postscript: "In a day or two I am going to Germany to see my mother and take a holiday. My nerves are worn to shreds and I am feeling quite ill." His vacation, certainly long overdue and badly needed, was spent on the coast of northern France rather than in Germany. His mother and sister Anna joined him there for almost a month.

Once back in London, Lenin again plunged into a heavy work load. Besides his normal duties with *Iskra* as editor, contributor, and supervising correspondent for the distribution network in Russia, he found time for political pamphlets and an occasional lecture. To this formidable schedule he added still another assignment: preparations for the forthcoming party congress. In mid-November of 1902 a conference theoretically representing various Social Democratic factions met in Pskov and formed an organizing committee. The members were largely *Iskra* supporters, for Lenin had done most of the preliminary work through his Russian contacts. But communication was slow and uncertain, and at times he despaired of ever creating a true Social Democratic party. Insomnia and "nerves" plagued him, reaching a climax in the spring of 1903 when he broke out with a rash on his back and chest. His ailment might have been shingles—a virus disease—but the circumstances suggest psychosomatic illness, then virtually an unknown concept to the medical profession. Krupskaya made a ludicrous diagnosis of ringworm after consulting a medical handbook and painted him with iodine, causing "excruciating pain."

Lenin's poor health was only partially due to the nervous strain occasioned by organizational problems. His relations with Martov, Zasulich, and Potresov, his *Iskra* colleagues residing in London, had cooled perceptibly, partly because his driving energy and secretive attitude about his Russian connections discouraged the less ambitious trio from closer collaboration. He had been particularly close to Martov, but the good-natured jests and the tone of intimacy were now missing. Sensing his growing isolation, he proposed the co-optation of Trotsky—by now a frequent contributor—as a member of the editorial board. Although Plekhanov vetoed the idea, Trotsky was nevertheless invited to editorial meetings in an "advisory" capacity. Several weeks later the board overrode Lenin's objections and decided to move *Iskra* to Geneva, supposedly because living costs were lower and contact with Russia easier. Early in May, while still in pain from his skin inflammation, Lenin made the difficult journey to Switzerland and was confined to bed for two weeks.

Lenin and Krupskaya rented a small house on the outskirts of Geneva. *Iskra* became less a one-man enterprise, but open disagreements were now more frequent, and the editorial board usually split evenly, with the "elders" (Plekhanov, Axelrod, and Zasulich) on one side and the "youngsters" (Lenin, Martov, and Potresov) on the other. The delegates to the forthcoming party congress began to trickle in, a few from the Russian underground but chiefly long-term expatriates. Once he regained his health, Lenin held a kind of "open house" as an active lobbyist for the *Iskra* faction. The loquacious Martov was also much in evidence, while Plekhanov retained his customary reserve but did invite several of the delegates for tea. Alexander Shotman, one of the few genuine workers among the preponderance of intellectuals who attended the subsequent congress, was disturbed by the bourgeois elegance of Plekhanov's quarters and felt more comfortable in the proletarian simplicity of Lenin's home.

On July 30, 1903, the grand climax to years of effort by the leaders of Russian Marxism at last became a reality. Fifty-seven delegates representing twenty-six organizations met in a vast flour warehouse in Brussels, and their intrusion, reports Krupskaya in a rare flash of humor, "only succeeded in astonishing the rats and the policemen." It was the founding congress of the Russian Social Democratic Labor Party, though in deference to the stillborn "first" congress at Minsk in 1898 it has been traditionally designated the "second." It was a momentous occasion to the participants, and especially to Lenin, but it attracted almost no attention from the European public. Except for afficionados of revolutionary history, it would have been forgotten but for the Bolshevik Revolution of 1917. This inconspicuous gathering of Russian socialists thus acquired in retrospect great historical significance. The honor of opening the proceedings was conferred on Plekhanov, who spoke briefly but with deep feeling. He was thereupon elected chairman by acclamation. Forty-three of the fifty-seven delegates possessed voting rights, and since eight had a double vote there were fifty-one votes in all. The *Iskra* faction commanded, at least on paper, thirty-three of the total, and others could be expected. The only other bloc of any consequence, the so-called Bund or Jewish Social Democratic organization, had five votes, far less than its membership warranted. The Economists, no longer a unified group, had only two or three sympathizers. It seemed evident therefore that the *Iskra* veterans were in complete control, yet the supreme irony of the occasion lay in the split of the majority along lines that had not been foreseen. Lenin arranged the agenda and formulated a set of party rules to be presented to the delegates. He continued to caucus behind the scenes in a series of private meetings, and in the early sessions, largely devoted to procedural wrangling, the Leninist steamroller encountered no more than token opposition.

Meanwhile the Belgian police, prompted by Russian diplomatic protests and Okhrana agents in Brussels, began to take an undue interest in the proceedings. Constant petty harassment culminated in four delegates being summarily ordered to leave the country. The congress had been unable—or perhaps unwilling because of security reasons—to obtain a permanent site, and the meetings were suspended on August 5 and resumed in a London church on August 11. There the Iskrites began to lose their cohesion—to divide, as Lenin put it later, into the "hards" and the "softs." His own conduct may have contributed to the cleavage, for his nerves were again keyed up, and Krupskaya reports, with pardonable exaggeration, that he stopped eating and sleeping altogether. Although he spoke briefly and infrequently at the earlier sessions, he was tactless and overbearing in private and needlessly antagonized his own supporters. He lost his first real test of strength on an item in the party rules defining membership. The formula he submitted followed the argument made in *What Is to Be Done?*—that is, the need to establish a tightly organized band of revolutionary conspirators. Martov's alternate proposal would extend membership to anyone who "accepts its program, supports the party by material means, and renders it regular personal assistance under the direction of one of the party organizations." The distinction was subtle—unnecessarily so for the repressive conditions then prevailing in Russia—and in any case less momentous than later commentators have contrived to make it. Lenin's version was defeated by twenty-eight votes to twenty-three, and it was this loss of his seemingly automatic majority that triggered further disputes and split the party asunder before it was properly launched.

Five Bundists helped pass Martov's proposal and then quit

the congress when their demand for autonomy within the party was denied. Two Economists also walked out, giving Lenin a narrow voting edge. In an extremity of self-righteousness, he mobilized his loyal following for the battles that lay ahead. Oddly enough, Plekhanov had sided with Lenin on the issue of party membership and continued to give him firm support. "Of such stuff Robespierres are made," he remarked in a complimentary but ironic vein about his former disciple.[10] Lenin used his new-found majority to ram through a new *Iskra* editorial board: Plekhanov, Martov, and himself, thus eliminating Axelrod, Zasulich, and Potresov, who had apparently gone over to the Martov "faction." That Martov refused to serve did not deter Lenin's determination that the "hards" should control the party. Three convinced but lesser known Leninists were elected as the Central Committee to supervise the underground apparatus in Russia. A five-man Party Council, two to be chosen by the *Iskra* board and two by the Central Committee, was to be the apex of the party structure, and with Plekhanov's selection as the fifth member (and chairman) of this body Lenin's victory seemed secure.

By August 23 the delegates were exhausted by the marathon sessions, the impassioned oratory, and the clash of temperament. The agenda was far from completed, but amid a spurious sense of solidarity on the eve of adjournment a series of innocuous resolutions passed unanimously. Lenin was prompt—as well as psychologically astute—in christening his followers "Bolsheviks" (majoritarians) and those of the opposition "Mensheviks" (minoritarians) , and it was typical of Martov's passivity and political ineptitude that he accepted the label without protest even when his collaborators regained control of the party.

The results of the congress bewildered the rank and file. Even the participants were aghast that party "unification" had led to a schism of such magnitude, nor did they agree as to precisely what had caused it. According to Trotsky, Lenin was sick for several weeks with a "nervous illness," and shortly afterward, while riding a bicycle in Geneva, he absentmindedly ran into a streetcar and badly injured an eye. Sobered by what had happened to the party, he tried to make amends. He confessed in a letter to Potresov that he had "often behaved and acted in a state of frightful irritation, 'frenziedly,'" and that he was quite willing to admit his fault to anyone. Nevertheless, he declared that he could detect "absolutely nothing" in his conduct that was injurious to the party or anything that was an affront or insult to the minority. But he made no direct overtures to Martov, and his erstwhile "best friend," the more personally bitter of the two, was indisposed toward a reconciliation. Plekhanov tried vainly to play the role of peacemaker ("Better a bullet in the head than a split"). Hoping to exert pressure on Lenin to allow the four former *Iskra* editors to return, he threatened to resign from the board. Lenin, in the interest of harmony (or so he maintained) and in the knowledge that the Bolsheviks controlled the Party Center and the Central Committee, resigned instead on November 1. It was to prove a major tactical error. Plekhanov recalled the four editors and, growing weary of Lenin's intransigence, gradually reversed the position he had taken at the recent congress. He now discovered "Bonapartist" tendencies in Lenin and charged that the Bolsheviks confused the "dictatorship of the proletariat with a dictatorship over the proletariat."[11]

Lenin's supposed lust for power and his unscrupulous means of achieving it is a refrain that many of his critics took up even before the Bolshevik Revolution. Later on, especially when the excesses of the Stalin dictatorship gave rise to a closer examination of the roots of Bolshevism, Western scholars found that the charge was not without merit. They purported to see a natural link between Lenin's dogmatism in political controversy and his concept of an elite party with the unsavory features of Soviet totalitarianism that have persisted to our own day. That a monolithic party and a repressive society did develop under Stalin was, of course, no whim of fate, but to view Lenin as a ruthless would-be dictator as far back as 1903 is to indulge too freely in the temptation of instant wisdom by hindsight. Like most of his associates, he accepted wholeheartedly Plekhanov's dictum that the "health of the revolution is the supreme law." He differed with the Mensheviks quite markedly on political tactics, and the success of his party in 1917 is certainly a major indication that he was right and they were wrong as far as revolutionary strategy is concerned. Revolutions are seldom—perhaps never—wholly spontaneous events. Leadership is the vital ingredient, and Lenin took it as something of a compliment when he and his fellow Bolsheviks were accused of being Jacobins. Some-

one, he argued, must take up the "conductor's baton." Should it
be Plekhanov? A "first-class scholar" but incapable of organizing
anything or anyone. Axelrod, Zasulich, Potresov? Too laughable
to talk about. Martov? An excellent journalist but a "hysterical
intellectual." Trotsky?! "Who is there? The rest are nobodies!
It's enough to make a cat laugh."[12] His unspoken conviction
that he deserved the conductor's baton was less a craving for
personal power than a kind of self-evident axiom: only he was
properly equipped to lead the party that would bring about the
revolution. And, to be thoroughly pragmatic, history was to prove
him right.

Lenin tried to mount a counteroffensive by repeating the
strategy that had been so successful in securing *Iskra's* domination
of the London congress. The local committees in Russia would be
won over to Bolshevism and persuaded to call for a new party
congress. The Central Committee, to which he had been co-opted,
proved unenthusiastic despite its Leninist composition. "All of
us implore the Old Man [Lenin] to give up his quarrel and
start working," five members wrote from Russia. "We are waiting
for leaflets, pamphlets, and all kinds of advice—the best way of
soothing one's nerves and answering slanders."[13] But Lenin stubbornly pursued his course, disregarding his virtual isolation in
the Central Committee and producing in the spring of 1904 a
substantial polemic against the Mensheviks: *One Step Forward,
Two Steps Back,* subtitled "The Crisis in Our Party." He went
over the melancholy events of the Second Congress in elaborate
detail, and for those outside the movement it must have had all
the charm and clarity of a tract on medieval theology. It contributed nothing essentially new to the debate, nor did the tone
commend itself to the opposition as a reasoned discussion of the
issues. But it was an aggressive and even powerful attack, certainly persuasive to Leninists and capable of attracting support
to the Bolshevik cause from those sufficiently motivated to read
it. However trenchant his language, Lenin did not descend to
personal abuse and carefully preserved the amenities (or was it
ironic politeness?) to "Comrade Martov," "Comrade Plekhanov,"
and—incredibly—"Comrade Bernstein."

During the summer of 1904 the Central Committee co-opted
three new members, nominally Mensheviks, and took other measures to place Lenin in political quarantine. Depressed and worn

out by the struggle, he sought the therapy of a month's walking tour in the Swiss mountains. He and Krupskaya slept outdoors, ate frugally, and read almost nothing. Refreshed—"his cheerful old self again"—Lenin laid plans for a newspaper to compete with *Iskra*. He had little money of his own, and his former sources of financial assistance had dried up or defected to the Mensheviks. But funds did materialize, possibly from the novelist Maxim Gorky, the eccentric industrialist Savva Morozov, and agents of the Japanese government (the Russo-Japanese War had begun early in the year).[14] Soviet historians have maintained uniform silence on this intriguing question. The first issue of Lenin's new Bolshevik organ *Vperyod* ("Forward"), appeared in Geneva on January 4, 1905. Later that month the notorious Bloody Sunday incident, in which hundreds of workers were killed or wounded in St. Petersburg while attempting to present a petition to the Tsar, set off a chain reaction that brought the monarchy to the brink of collapse.

CHAPTER IV

The Abortive Revolution

BOLSHEVISM, WHICH FIRST SAW THE LIGHT OF DAY IN 1903, WAS essentially Leninism writ large. Its impact during the Revolution of 1905—as that of Menshevism—was ephemeral but not entirely superficial. The party followed rather than led events, and the only Social Democrat to play a conspicuous role was Trotsky, who had turned away from Lenin after the Second Congress but failed to find a congenial sanctuary with the Mensheviks. He and Plekhanov had conceived a mutual dislike, and his friendship with Martov did not survive the testing time of 1905. Lenin, whose own stature was not appreciably enhanced by the revolutionary year, generously conceded that Trotsky's reputation was based on his "tireless and striking work."

When news of Bloody Sunday reached Geneva, Lenin and his wife were headed for the library. "Instinct drew us, together with all the other Bolsheviks . . . to the emigrants' restaurant kept by the Lepeshinskys," Krupskaya reports. "The realization came over everyone in a wave that the revolution had begun, that the shackles of faith in the tsar had been torn apart, and the hour was near when 'tyranny shall fall, and the people shall rise up, great, powerful and free.'" Father Gapon, the politically naive priest who had led the ill-fated procession to the Winter Palace, fled the country and soon arrived in Geneva. He was lionized by the Socialist Revolutionaries, the political successors of the old Populists, and for a time flirted with the Social Democrats. Lenin correctly surmised that he had been an *agent provocateur* but allowed for the possibility that he might be a "sincere Christian Socialist and that it was Bloody Sunday which converted him to the true revolutionary path." For the time being Social Democrats should maintain a "cautious, guarded, skeptical attitude" toward him.[1]

An instant revolutionary whom fate had thrust into an unac-

customed role, Gapon expressed a desire to meet the local Marxist
celebrities. Plekhanov, typically, gave him a cool reception, but
Lenin, always eager to probe the psychology of the masses, no
matter how indirectly, recognized his popular appeal and sensed
his possible usefulness. A meeting was arranged in a "neutral"
cafe, and he supposedly told Gapon, "Don't you listen to flattery,
my dear man. If you don't study, that is where you'll be"—and
he pointed under the table. But Gapon sought crowds and ex-
citement, not book learning or political debate. He lent his name
to a poorly managed gun-running project in which a small steam-
ship, the *John Grafton,* attempted to convey a cargo of arms and
ammunition from England to Russia. It ran aground off the
coast of Finland, and Bolshevik agents, though uninvolved with
the original venture, sought a share in the salvage operation,
apparently without success. Gapon returned to Russia and eventually resumed his police contacts. As a traitor to the revolution
he was killed by Socialist Revolutionaries in 1906.

Although excited by the revolutionary possibilities that loomed
up so suddenly and constantly bombarding his followers in Russia with inflammatory exhortations, Lenin was not disposed to
hasten his return. The reasons are not clear, but apparently he
considered it a risky enterprise until a political amnesty in the
fall overcame his hesitation. Meanwhile a Bolshevik conference
convened in London (April 25–May 10, 1905), audaciously referred to by Soviet historians as the Third Party Congress. It met
at Lenin's behest (though his role was disguised) with a shallow
pretense that it represented the mandate of a united party. No
Mensheviks were invited—they improvised their own conference
in Geneva—but the disciplined band of followers that Lenin
anticipated did not quite materialize. For the most part advocates
of party unity, the delegates shied away from his aggressive stand
against the "traitorous" Mensheviks, and he was forced to remain
content with compromise resolutions that kept the door ajar
for the errant party "comrades." The Bolshevik chieftain nevertheless emerged with a more dynamic image than either Martov
or Plekhanov, and his prestige obviously exceeded that of the
year before when his political fortunes had reached a new low.
During the summer, perhaps reflecting his own mood, he complained in a letter to Anatole Lunacharsky, a Bolshevik colleague
in Italy, that "our people in Geneva are down in the dumps,"

whereas "the Iskrites are lively and bustling, brazen as hucksters, skilled by long experience in demagogy." "Among our people," he went on, "a kind of 'conscientious stupidity' or 'stupid con-scientiousness' prevails. They can't put up a fight, they're clumsy, inactive, awkward, timid. . . . Good fellows, but damned worth-less as politicians."[2]

Lenin's expectation of an armed uprising against the tsarist regime was keyed to his reliance upon conspiratorial tactics and party discipline. The Bolsheviks were distrustful of working class spontaneity and vainly sought to harness the discontent and grow-ing militance of the masses. The Mensheviks, less doctrinaire about proper revolutionary procedure, were no more successful in directing the course of events but did cooperate with the St. Petersburg Soviet of Workers' Deputies, a kind of strike com-mittee that quickly assumed governmental functions in the fall of 1905. Its founders and leaders were chiefly Mensheviks, but Lenin's suspicion of the organization (after a favorable initial impression) was based partly on its reluctance to press on toward what he deemed the immediate task—armed insurrection. His only extended comment on the Soviet, written in mid-November from "that accursed afar, that hateful 'abroad' of an émigré," recommended that it be considered the nucleus of a *"provisional revolutionary government."*[3] These remarks were never published until "found" in 1940, and it seems probable that Lenin con-sidered them indiscreet after returning to Russia and encounter-ing opposition from his followers. His retrospective opinion of the Soviet was generally sympathetic, though he remained tem-peramentally incapable of ascribing great merit to any movement so obviously independent of Bolshevik influence. He likewise failed to provide a pat formula to appraise the wholly unexpected general strike that paralyzed the country and induced the Tsar to grant an embryo constitution on October 30.

After a two-week delay in Stockholm, supposedly caused by the failure of his contact to supply him with false identity papers, Lenin finally reached the Russian capital on November 21, 1905. By this time the revolutionary tide had begun to recede. The euphoria generated by a successful struggle with the autocracy gradually faded as the government, led by the newly appointed Sergei Witte as chairman of the Council of Ministers, regained the initiative. The unpopular war with Japan had ended in

September with the signing of the Treaty of Portsmouth, a lenient peace considering Russia's unbroken series of military and naval defeats. The ranks of the militant grew thin as the liberal bourgeoisie and a sizable section of the working class deserted the revolutionary cause, placated by the promise of civil liberties and a national assembly. Symptomatic of the growing reaction, the "patriotic" and ultra-nationalist Black Hundreds— a foreshadowing of the European fascist gangs of the 1920s— launched a campaign of terror and assassination against intellectuals, revolutionaries, Jews, and other non-Russian minorities.

Lenin's role was essentially that of a spectator, for he was not a member of the Soviet, and the Bolsheviks had no mass following that could be galvanized into action. He became an editor and contributor to *Novaya zhizn* ("New Life"), the legal Bolshevik newspaper backed by Maxim Gorky, whose common-law wife was the publisher of record. It was a modest post in the light of his later renown, and Soviet historians have busied themselves in fashioning a more appropriate but wholly anachronistic legend to fill the void of 1905. But the latest "official" biography is content to ignore previous claims that he contrived to direct the Soviet from behind the scenes.[4]

On December 16 the government ringed the St. Petersburg Soviet with police and picked troops and arrested the deputies. The response—another general strike—aroused more enthusiasm than might have been expected in view of the economic privation and emotional exhaustion occasioned by the one so recently ended. But the necessary mass participation could not be sustained a second time. In Moscow, however, barricades were thrown up on major boulevards and guerrilla warfare broke out. Although the rebellion had no prospect of success, reliable troops had to be brought in to subdue the tenacious insurgents. Since the local Bolsheviks were the most prominent group in organizing the uprising, it would be a natural assumption that Lenin was directly involved in the affair. But that he gave explicit orders to his followers in Moscow appears unlikely even though his position on the necessity of armed rebellion was clear enough. He was attending a Bolshevik conference in Tammerfors, Finland, during the peak of the fighting, evidence, though admittedly tentative, that he anticipated no immediate outbreak in Moscow.

The post mortem was inconclusive and even spiteful. The

Bolsheviks tended to blame the Mensheviks for weakness and irresolution, while the latter charged that their Social Democratic colleagues had been hasty and impetuous. Lenin managed, at least in his published writings, to mask his keen disappointment, claiming that the workers had learned valuable lessons. Contrary to Plekhanov's view, "seized upon by all the opportunists," that the uprising was ill-advised, Lenin declared that the revolutionaries "should have taken up arms more resolutely, energetically, and aggressively." "A great mass struggle is approaching," he maintained in the late summer of 1906 when revolutionary fervor had reached its nadir. "The masses must know that they are entering upon an armed, bloody, and desperate struggle. . . . The offensive against the enemy must be pressed with the greatest vigor."⁵ The experience of 1905 was to be but a "dress rehearsal" for the final reckoning with the tsarist autocracy.

Lenin lived clandestinely in St. Petersburg, reluctantly—to please his adherents—denouncing the forthcoming elections to the Duma as a sham. The Socialist Revolutionaries as well as the Bolsheviks officially boycotted the election campaign. The Mensheviks declared their original opposition a mistake and elected twelve deputies from Transcaucasia, traditionally an area of strong support for their faction. Only many years later did Lenin publicly confess that the boycott had been a major error.

In the spring of 1906, at the time of the Duma elections, the revolutionaries were still prisoners of their combat psychology. Very few admitted, even to themselves, that the masses had temporarily abandoned the political struggle. The Social Democrats foresaw a new confrontation at any time and sought to prepare for it by convening a so-called "unification congress" in Stockholm (April 10–25, 1906). Lenin was unusually conciliatory despite the inferiority of his bargaining position: of the 111 voting delegates 62 were Mensheviks and no more than 46 Bolsheviks. The nearly unanimous sentiment among his followers for a united party probably had more to do with his willingness to compromise than a mellowed personality or altered opinions. Martov and Trotsky were absent—both had been arrested in Russia—but most of the other Social Democratic luminaries attended, Plekhanov included.

The delegates did indeed achieve a certain bogus unity—not that they were hypocritical in their stated desire for a united front against the common enemy. But Lenin hardly contemplated the dissolution of the party apparatus that he had so carefully nurtured, and it is difficult to see in the Stockholm congress the kind of genuine and permanent rapport that would heal the wounds of personal and ideological recrimination. The Menshevik majority, however, did not ride roughshod over the Bolshevik minority, nor did their delegates always agree among themselves. They split, for example, on the issue seemingly so vital in 1903—that of defining party membership—allowing Lenin's formula to prevail. But his agrarian platform, calling for the nationalization of the land, met defeat in favor of the Menshevik resolution for "municipalization"—that is, local control through democratic elections. This disagreement on the land question was to acquire decisive significance in 1917; and even in 1906 the peasants, generally dismissed in Marxist theory as a property-minded "petty bourgeois" element, were still demonstrating in various parts of the empire that their insatiable land hunger could be an important weapon in the revolutionary arsenal. Lenin, so Krupskaya relates, conceived the notion of a "radical" solution to the agrarian problem in 1905 after talks with Gapon and a young sailor of peasant origin who had been one of the ringleaders in the mutiny aboard the battleship *Potemkin*. The Bolshevik program had timidly advocated a return of the "cut offs"—land taken from the peasants by the landlords at the time of the emancipation of the serfs in 1861. Henceforth the demand was made for the confiscation of *all* the land. But neither at Stockholm in 1906 nor on later occasions did the Bolsheviks seek to clarify the studied ambiguity of their prescription. To do so would have alienated the peasants: on the one hand they were welcomed into the revolutionary fold with a seemingly unqualified promise that the land was theirs for the taking; on the other, since they were small-scale capitalists and potential enemies of socialism their land was subject to future expropriation by the state.

Lenin returned to St. Petersburg fully expecting new revolutionary outbreaks. But public apathy was broken only by the novelty of the First Duma, which opened on May 10 with a large plurality of deputies representing the liberal Constitutional Democrats (Kadets) . Consistent with his astringent view of bourgeois liberalism, Lenin wrote contemptuously of the party as "good for nothing better than toy-parliament oratory," although the "petty bourgeois voters" who supported them contained "many advanced and potentially militant democratic elements."[6] On May 22, using the name Karpov, he addressed a mass meeting for the first time in his career. "Terribly agitated" and "very pale," he spoke at a "people's palace" founded by Countess Sofia Panina, a liberal humanitarian and social worker. According to Krupskaya, his inaugural appearance as a non-party agitator was received with "extraordinary enthusiasm," and the crowd dispersed singing revolutionary songs. He spoke at other semipublic rallies during the next few weeks and remained a firm opponent of the Duma for debauching the "revolutionary consciousness of the people." Since the Tsar also deplored the Duma's pernicious influence—obviously for different reasons— the Okhrana gave the Bolsheviks free rein in their campaign to discredit the new assembly. Lenin's extraordinary immunity from arrest in 1906 may be explained in large part by this temporary and unacknowledged "alliance."

The "unified" Social Democratic Party was ostensibly directed by a Menshevik-dominated Central Committee. But Lenin maintained a secret Bolshevik "center" and soon gained a majority on the St. Petersburg Committee. After the dissolution of the Duma on July 21, 1906, he reversed his previous position, now arguing that it was a valuable forum for agitation. He recommended full Social Democratic participation in the forthcoming elections to the Second Duma. A conference at Tammerfors near the end of the year provided that local party organizations might support other candidates, even Kadets, when it was deemed necessary to defeat the nominees of the extreme Right. This delegation of authority worked fairly well, for most of the provincial leaders were genuinely anxious for party harmony and did their best to carry out the Tammerfors mandate. But Lenin had not altered his opinion that the Kadets were "counterrevolutionary," and in St. Petersburg he mobilized his followers to form a "Left bloc" against them. The local Mensheviks protested and formed their own bloc, including the Kadets. Lenin responded with a polemic in pamphlet form accusing the Mensheviks of sordid bargaining with the Kadets in order to obtain a seat in the Duma ("The Mensheviks claim that they fear a Black Hundred danger in St. Petersburg. . . . This is sheer hypocrisy, designed to conceal the haggling of the petty bourgeois section of the workers' party over a miserable seat in the Duma, begged from the Kadets") .[7] The episode reveals the most disagreeable and contumacious side of Lenin's nature: wholly convinced of his own political sagacity and moral rectitude yet unwilling to acknowledge that dissenters could be moved by anything other than sordid motives.

The party's Central Committee, exasperated by Lenin's conduct, convened a "court of honor" in the spring of 1907 to hear charges that he had slandered his colleagues. Composed of three Mensheviks, three of Lenin's appointees, and three "neutrals" representing the Lettish, Polish, and Jewish Social Democrats, the tribunal held only two meetings and then adjourned to prepare for the forthcoming party congress. It rendered no verdict, nor did it resume the hearing at a more propitious time, for the Bolsheviks regained their majority status in the interim. Lenin's self-righteousness and aggressive debating style may be gauged by the statement he made to the "comrade judges" in his own defense: "The wording [of the pamphlet attacking the Mensheviks] is calculated to evoke in the reader hatred, disgust, and contempt for people who do such things. . . . [It] is calculated not to convince but to break up the ranks of the opponent, not to correct his mistakes but to destroy him, to wipe his organization off the face of the earth." "I am told," he went on, "you have spread discord in the ranks of the proletariat. My answer is: I purposely and deliberately spread discord in the ranks of that section of the Petersburg proletariat which followed the Mensheviks . . . *and I shall always* act in that way *whenever a split occurs.*"[8] He thus served ample notice, with refreshing but insolent candor, of what his fellow Social Democrats could expect if they strayed from his conception of ideological and tactical purity.

Since the late summer of 1906 Lenin had found it expedient to live in Kuokkala, Finland, near the Russian frontier, where he was reasonably secure from the attentions of the secret police. Krupskaya commuted to St. Petersburg almost daily, and a special courier brought Lenin his mail and picked up his articles for *Proletary* ("The Proletarian") , the illegal continuation of previous Bolshevik newspapers. But he fretted in his relative isolation, and the large "family" of revolutionaries—they lived in the rambling country house of a fellow Bolshevik—occasionally diverted him from spells of moodiness by playing *doorak,* a Russian card game ("Ilyich," says Krupskaya, "played with careful zest").

In April, 1907, Lenin left for Copenhagen to attend the Fifth Party Congress. He was determined to reverse the minority position of the Bolsheviks, while the Mensheviks reluctantly (and against Plekhanov's advice) consented to attend another congress in the hope that the party could achieve the genuine spirit of unity that had proved so elusive at Stockholm the year before. The Danish authorities, under pressure from the Russian government, gave summary notice that the delegates were not welcome in Copenhagen and, as in 1903, the meeting was transferred to London. Reflecting Lenin's tireless work and superior financial resources, the Bolsheviks commanded a slight majority—actually only a plurality—of the voting delegates, who claimed to represent a party membership of 147,000. Procedural arguments and other technicalities delayed the proceedings even more than was customary for a sizable group of voluble Russians, and the congress dragged on from May 13 to June 1 in a Christian Socialist church.

The Bolshevik majority was unstable, and Lenin failed to attain the crushing victory that he so eagerly anticipated. Nor did he dominate the newly elected Central Committee. It contained five Bolsheviks to four Mensheviks, but the balance of power lay with the "national" affiliates (Letts, Poles, and Jews) and their six members. Nevertheless, it became evident during the congress, as it had been for some time before, that the caliber of leadership that Lenin provided for his faction was sorely lacking in the case of the Mensheviks. Martov, their "official" spokesman, was present for the occasion and an effective if somewhat histrionic debater, yet he retained his "soft" image of vacillation and faintheartedness. Trotsky, who escaped from his Siberian exile in time for the congress, records in his autobiography that Martov, suffering from neurasthenia or some kind of mental fatigue in 1906, was at a loss as to what to call his illness. It definitely had a name, declares Trotsky, unable to resist a malicious quip: "Menshevism." Plekhanov also attended but was less inclined than ever to depart from his carefully cultivated pose of the wise elder statesman, above the sordid business of factional strife.

Lenin's most resounding defeat came on the question of "expropriations" or—to discard the euphemism favored by the revolutionaries—armed robbery. With the party exchequer seriously depleted, the temptation to indulge in unorthodox—indeed criminal—methods of fund raising was hard to resist. Banks were the prime target, but occasionally a wealthy individual might be victimized. Lenin, if not wholly enthusiastic about such tactics, was never squeamish about the source of his revenue and did not discourage his more daring followers. Martov, among others, later maintained that the Bolshevik majority at London had been obtained because of vast resources acquired through expropriations and other unsavory means. A resolution condemned "partisan attacks" and prohibited party members from engaging in such activities. Yet the most notorious expropriation occurred only a few weeks later when a daring holdup of funds being transferred to the state bank in Tiflis yielded 341,000 rubles, theoretically a great windfall for the Bolsheviks. But nearly all the banknotes were in five-hundred-ruble denominations, and most of the agents who tried to cash them in European banks were arrested. According to a legend which may have some basis in fact, Joseph Stalin, then an obscure Caucasian Bolshevik, masterminded the whole affair.

In London, meanwhile, the party delegates faced an immediate financial crisis. The prolonged congress had consumed the money available for transportation home, and a special committee cast about for likely sources of assistance. The prospects looked bleak until English sympathizers contacted Joseph Fels, a wealthy American businessman (of the Fels-Naphtha soap empire) known for his interest in social reform and humanitarian causes. He attended a session of the congress and, though knowing no Russian, was suitably impressed by the sincerity of the participants. He granted a loan of £1,700 without interest, and most of the delegates (Lenin was not among them) duly signed a note promising repayment by January 1, 1908. But the party soon fell upon evil days. Fels died in 1914 without recovering his money—he had insisted upon reimbursement, apparently regretting his generosity —but in 1922 his widow was paid in full by the Soviet trade delegation in London.[9]

Lenin returned in a state of nervous exhaustion, and to Krupskaya, who had remained in Finland, he looked rather odd:

beardless, with his mustache clipped short, and wearing a big straw hat. After proper rest, fresh air, exercise, and a diet of "nourishing omelettes and deer ham," he became his old self again.[10]

On June 3, 1907, before Lenin reached Finland, the government dismissed the Second Duma, charging the Social Democratic deputies with a plot to undermine the loyalty of the armed forces. A new electoral law weighted the vote in favor of the well-to-do, an illegal act since the Duma had not been consulted. Many revolutionaries were arrested, including most of the Social Democratic deputies. The latter were tried secretly, and the majority received prison terms or were sent into administrative exile. Much of the evidence was manufactured by a police agent, but subversion, however defined, had indeed been the chief occupation of the Social Democrats as well as the Socialist Revolutionaries. Lenin, who had prodded his Duma faction of eighteen to make more incendiary remarks and had even written some of the speeches himself, remained unperturbed. He thought the affair might help to dispel the constitutional illusions of the masses, although his view of the "parliamentary comic opera" had grown less contemptuous as he came to appreciate the agitational and propaganda advantages that the Duma offered.

Knowing that the Third Duma would be thoroughly reactionary, Lenin persisted, in the face of heavy opposition from his own followers, in advocating an energetic election campaign. In August, at a party conference in Finland, he was the only Bolshevik to vote with the Mensheviks on the question, an embarrassing example of opportunism to his chief aide, Alexander Bogdanov. Thereafter their relationship cooled, and Bogdanov eventually left the Bolshevik fold altogether. The Social Democratic representation in the Third Duma fell to eighteen, of whom only five were Bolsheviks (and one of these a police agent). The group as a whole was not noted for its aggressiveness —they were mindful of the fate of their predecessors—but considering the lowly state of the party during the next decade it mattered little whether Lenin's strategy of participation prevailed over that of the boycott.

In August, 1907, Lenin attended the congress of the Second (Socialist) International in Stuttgart. There he had a first-hand opportunity to observe far more outrageous examples of heresy and treachery than the Mensheviks could ever have contrived. Even Bernstein, an admitted renegade in Lenin's eyes, was treated with the respect due a leading socialist theoretician. Not many of the Western delegates, urbane and cosmopolitan intellectuals almost to a man, were conversant with the obscure and distant squabbles of the Russian Marxists, and few of these could really comprehend what the issues were all about. A somewhat patronizing attitude, particularly among the venerable German Social Democrats, seemed to imply that a semi-barbaric land such as Russia must logically produce strange and outlandish doctrines.

Finland's seeming immunity from the tsarist police had become doubtful by the time of Lenin's return from Stuttgart. But he remained at Kuokkala for several months, traveling freely about the country as necessity arose. By November of 1907, when continued residence in Finland became hazardous, he moved farther from St. Petersburg. Finally convinced that the autocracy had reestablished its authority for an indefinite period, he decided to emigrate once more. Toward the end of the year he set out for Åbo to take the steamer to Sweden. Leaving the train some miles short of his destination to avoid suspected police detectives, he trudged the rest of the way in bitter cold. He missed the boat at Åbo but caught it at a nearby island, nearly losing his life in the process. On the long walk to the embarkation point the ice gave way, and he and his rather inebriated escort of two local peasants barely managed to save themselves. His first thought, he recalled later, was "Ah, what a stupid way to die."[11]

Krupskaya joined her husband in Stockholm, and they returned to Geneva after spending a few days in Berlin. Their stay in the German capital was a mixed pleasure, for both were laid low by food poisoning. But Lenin had an opportunity to renew his acquaintance with Rosa Luxemburg, the Polish-born Marxist with whom he had gotten along famously at the Stuttgart congress. They arrived at their destination in the dead of winter— January of 1908—and as they walked through the cold and desolate streets of Geneva, Lenin remarked forebodingly, "I have a feeling as if I've come here to be buried."[12]

CHAPTER V

The Second Emigration

ALMOST A DECADE WAS TO PASS BEFORE LENIN RETURNED TO HIS homeland. That it would ever be possible seemed unlikely, either in 1908 or the years that followed. Even the most optimistic revolutionary could find little comfort in the news from Russia: reaction sat enthroned, not simply in the person of Nicholas II but in a governmental system—and a way of life—that seemed to survive the shock of 1905 with no visible change. Such was not quite the case. The Duma, for example, however disappointing as a parliamentary institution, at least functioned after a fashion. But public apathy was so profound and so nearly pervasive that it discouraged what little enthusiasm the revolutionaries could muster. In 1910 the Social Democrats numbered no more than 10,000—probably an inflated estimate—while only five or six Bolshevik committees were said to be functioning in the whole of the Russian empire.

For the expatriates, cut off from any effective participation in what now masqueraded as the "revolutionary struggle," these were years of frustration and despair. Secure from the danger of arrest and prison, they were nevertheless victims of circumstance, a prey to self-doubt and defeatism, buffeted by economic hardship, and subject to frayed nerves that frequently took the form of political backbiting and internecine feuds. They suffered, in short, from émigré neurosis, a psychic malaise for which idle revolutionaries might be said to have a special propensity.

Lenin's merits, once so obvious to his friends and well-wishers, now seemed questionable. The Mensheviks virtually wrote him off as a political cipher. His anxiety and insecurity—outwardly he was as self-assured as ever—sometimes flawed his judgment, and his stubborn dogmatism came to the fore when tactful diplomacy or political expediency would seem to have been the preferred method. But he scorned finesse and compromise, apparently as a matter of principle, and salvaged the remnants of his organization, determined to be ready if and when the next turn in history's wheel of fortune beckoned him to Russia once more.

The immediate task at hand was to relocate *Proletary*. Ostensibly the illegal Bolshevik organ (it bore a Moscow imprint to confuse the authorities) was published from September, 1906, to December, 1909. But of the fifty issues that appeared only the first twenty were actually printed in Russia. Geneva was too far from the Russian border to facilitate the arduous smuggling operation, but publication anywhere else would have raised even greater problems. By February, 1908, all the preliminary arrangements were made, and Lenin cautiously sounded out possible contributors, both financial and literary. Gorky and Trotsky, among others, were invited to write for the transplanted Bolshevik organ. The latter, with whom Lenin had exchanged harsh words after the party split in 1903, replied from Vienna through an intermediary that he was too busy. Lenin considered his refusal "mere posturing," recalling that he had acted the *"poseur"* at the recent London congress.[1]

Lenin had difficulty settling down to prosaic editorial duties. He spoke of *Proletary* as an "uncared-for waif" for which he dashed off articles in "incredible haste." Much of his time was spent at his "club"—a local reading room and library, where he allegedly consumed "whole days reading the accursed Machists." His uncomplimentary reference was to Ernst Mach (and his supposed disciples), a contemporary Austrian physicist and philosopher who specialized in epistemology. Lenin, who had displayed only casual interest in the more arcane branches of philosophy—the forthright and uncomplicated materialism of Marx and Engels was good enough for him—now became an "expert" on sense perception and other aspects of the theory of knowledge. His sudden concern with "Machism" was—predictably—less scholarly than political, for his relations with Bogdanov, who was on the editorial board of *Proletary*, had become strained. Bogdanov, a highly cultured Bolshevik with broad intellectual interests unrelated to politics, had published a three-volume work entitled *Empiriomonism* (1904–06) in which Mach's influence was apparent. Lenin, while agreeing with Plekhanov that the first volume was a "deviation" from Marxism, had nevertheless formed a "bloc" with Bogdanov in 1904, tacitly

ruling out philosophy as neutral ground. When the author presented him with the third volume in 1906, shortly after emerging
from a tsarist prison, Lenin read it at once and became "enraged."
"I then wrote him a 'declaration of love,'" he explained to
Gorky, "a letter on philosophy filling three notebooks."[2] He considered publishing his "letter" as "Notes of an Ordinary Marxist
Philosopher" but never got around to it. The notebooks were
left in St. Petersburg and were apparently lost.

Since Lenin admitted that it would be "unpardonable folly"
to split over the abstruse question of "materialism or Machism,"
why did he do just that in the summer of 1908 when Bogdanov
was ousted from the editorial board? One possible answer lies in
the unfortunate timing of a symposium, *Studies in the Philosophy of Marxism,* to which Bogdanov and others (including
two Mensheviks) contributed. It appeared while Lenin was working himself into a lather of righteous indignation over Bogdanov's "Machism," and he seized upon this fresh indiscretion as
evidence that his colleague had gone beyond the pale of socialist
respectability. "We ordinary Marxists are not well read in philosophy," he admitted, "but why insult us by serving this stuff
up to us as the philosophy of Marxism! I would sooner let myself
be drawn and quartered than consent to collaborate in an organ
or with a group that preaches such things." "One day I read one
of the empirio-critics and swear like a fishwife," he complained
to Gorky, and the "next day I read another and become ob-
scene."[3]

If Lenin considered Bogdanov's essay the last straw in a continuing ideological controversy, it is curious that his relationship
to Leonid Krasin, another close associate who bore no taint of
philosophical heresy, deteriorated at the same time. It has been
suggested that a more fundamental cause of the dispute involved
a disagreement over disbursing the proceeds of the Tiflis robbery
of 1907.[4] Both Bogdanov and Krasin had been instrumental in
supervising the expropriation policy, which Lenin had now discarded, and were the appointed guardians of the secret Bolshevik
treasury until replaced in August, 1908, by a new financial
commission headed by Gregory Zinoviev, Lenin's new "chief
executive."

Lenin bent over backward to preserve his friendship with
Gorky, who had close ties with Bogdanov and could easily have

been accused of ideological misdeeds. But Gorky was a writer of international renown with contacts and financial sources very useful to the Bolsheviks, and in any event Lenin considered literary artists a special breed, entitled to a certain degree of eccentricity on matters of doctrine. Although pleading lack of time and money, at the end of April, 1908, he finally accepted Gorky's repeated invitation to visit him on Capri near Naples. Bogdanov was already living there, along with two other Bolshevik "heretics," Anatole Lunacharsky and Vladimir Bazarov. Lenin was reticent about his trip, other than its scenic aspects, but seems to have parted on unfriendly terms with Bogdanov and his two associates while retaining in some degree his rapport with Gorky.

After returning to Geneva, Lenin went on to London, where he studied at the British Museum for several weeks and gathered material for a forthcoming philosophical bombshell that would presumably demolish the Machists and their ilk. His lengthy treatise was published in Moscow in the spring of 1909 under his old pseudonym "Vl. Ilyin" and bore the title *Materialism and Empiriocriticism: Critical Comments on a Reactionary Philosophy*. Revered in the Soviet Union as a Marxist classic only because Lenin wrote it, the book easily marks the low point of his literary career, though one may admire the pedantic industry with which he culled the major works of modern philosophy as well as the lesser products of the Machist school. Its tedium is relieved only by a vituperative style, and even this superficial liveliness tends to pall under a steady barrage of names, quotations, and *ad hominem* remarks. Like the treatises of medieval scholasticism, the reasoning is based on authority, and naturally the infallible oracles are Marx and Engels. Yet Marx had so seldom delved into pure philosophy that an appropriate quotation from Engels (whose canon was more relevant to the subject) is deemed sufficient to clinch the argument. This neglect of Marx, suggests one biographer, is akin to that of the Christian "who forever quotes Paul but finds no use for the words of Christ."[5] Mach himself is "exposed" as a plagiarist, while Bogdanov (with some attention to Bazarov and Lunacharsky) receives the brunt of Lenin's "quotational shock treatment," as Bogdanov himself labeled the method in rebuttal.

Lenin had a knack for coining (or borrowing) invidious terms for his opponents and their ideas. "Machism" was among the least successful of his creations, for the expression itself failed to evoke a negative image. But "God-seeking" and "God-building" were phrases that conveyed, at least to the revolutionaries, the desired flavor of ideological gaminess, and it was Lunacharsky's misfortune that his fumbling effort to create a secular "religion" received this unwelcome distinction. Along with Bogdanov and others, he was also guilty, in Lenin's estimation, of tactical errors that earned for the whole group two other uncomplimentary labels—"Ultimatists" and "Recallists." These ultra-leftists within the Bolshevik organization took a consistently critical view of the overly cautious Social Democratic deputies in the Third Duma and, while not advocates of "recalling" them, did insist that an "ultimatum" be sent to remind them of their revolutionary duty.

For a variety of reasons therefore—political, ideological, and personal—Lenin made a clean sweep of these malcontents at a conference of his followers in June, 1909. Expelled from the Bolshevik faction, they formed an opposition group under Bogdanov's leadership and took the name *Vperyod* in reference to the first Bolshevik newspaper. Besides sharing a kind of "leftist" revolutionary mystique and demonstrating varying degrees of distrust toward Lenin, the group had little in common. Under Gorky's patronage Bogdanov founded a Marxist school at Capri in August. Lenin was invited to lecture but declined, suggesting that Paris, where he had moved the previous winter, would be a more appropriate place for a "real" party school. The "Vperyodists" remained a small splinter group, though they did include many talented if decidedly unconventional Bolsheviks at a time when Lenin needed all the manpower he could muster to hold the organization together. Within a few years, having lost their cohesion, they split into two groups, and with the notable exception of Bogdanov most of the one time "Vperyodists" drifted back to the Leninist camp during World War I.

The Mensheviks were not forgotten while Lenin presided over the excommunication proceedings in his own ranks. He insisted that they were "Liquidators," seeking to dismantle the underground apparatus and to confine the party's activities to the legally permissible. The charge was largely a distortion for propaganda purposes, although Social Democrats of all persuasions had grown weary and despondent, and the Mensheviks had traditionally tended to welcome if not emphasize legal party work. Even without Lenin's nefarious "Liquidators" boring from within, the party was gradually "liquidating" itself.

Lenin's move to Paris (along with *Proletary*) had been made in the conviction that the "provincial backwater" of Geneva offered few intellectual and political opportunities as compared to a great metropolis. But the clinching argument, Krupskaya reports, was the claim of two visiting comrades from Paris that the Okhrana would be less likely to keep him under surveillance in a big city. One of these persuasive visitors was Dr. Jacob Zhitomirsky, an astute police agent who was fully aware that the tsarist government could ill afford an intelligence network in every émigré hideaway in Europe.

Lenin soon regretted his decision, not because of undue difficulty with the police but because Paris ("a rotten hole in many respects") came to symbolize his most trying years abroad. Prepared to read every sign and portent as a revolutionary awakening, even he grew discouraged. Nor was he in the best of health. Stomach trouble, insomnia, and headaches testified to his spiritual discomfort. Personal irritations also tended to exacerbate his general discontent: the Bibliothèque Nationale was too far from his residence for easy access, and its rules and regulations were designed less for the convenience of its readers than for its guardians. He used a bicycle for transportation, and on one occasion he was nearly run over by an automobile. Although he escaped unscathed, his bicycle was less fortunate, and in the end it (or a replacement) was stolen. Understandably, he would complain to Krupskaya, "What the devil made us go to Paris!"

Lenin's iron grip on the Bolshevik faction was deceptive, for it was the labor of Sisyphus to root out heresy in all its manifestations. No sooner had one group been ousted when another took its place. The "Conciliators" now demanded, partly in response to a groundswell of sentiment in what remained of the underground party, an end to the inquisition. They maintained that the Mensheviks, "Liquidators" or not, should be welcomed as fellow Social Democrats. Outnumbered, Lenin grudgingly consented to a plenary session of the Central Committee in Paris early in 1910. It was, he reported to Gorky, "three weeks of agony," of "squabbling, rows, and nervous strain." Again "compromise" and "unity" were achieved, but to Lenin vital principles had been sacrificed. He was forced to give up *Proletary* in favor of the non-factional *Sotsial-Demokrat;* to agree to a subsidy for *Pravda,* the "neutral" organ published by "that windbag Trotsky" in Vienna; to recognize the "Vperyodists" as a "literary group"; and, finally, on money matters, to consent to burn the remaining five-hundred-ruble notes taken in the Tiflis robbery and to share what was left of the notorious "Schmidt inheritance."

Nikolai Schmidt, a wealthy young man related to the Morozov family, had left a sizable fortune to the party upon his death in 1906. But his two sisters, perhaps with a better legal claim, acquired the money, whereupon Lenin dispatched Bolshevik agents to woo the young ladies. One of his emissaries married the older sister and proved reluctant to share his newfound affluence until threats of violence converted him to more tractable ways. The other, more trustworthy, became the younger sister's lover, skillfully detached her inheritance, and turned over the proceeds to the Bolshevik treasury. The total sum amounted to about 280,000 rubles ($140,000).

Lenin proceeded to ignore the spirit—and much of the substance—of the Paris conference. Protests notwithstanding, he held on to the Schmidt money (or most of it) as the argument over its proper disposition dragged on for years. *Proletary* did indeed cease publication, but *Sotsial-Demokrat* virtually replaced it as the Bolshevik organ when Lenin managed to gain a majority on the editorial board. Even the subsidy to *Pravda,* paid for a time, was withdrawn. Lenin's hostility toward Trotsky, shared by Plekhanov, was helpful in reviving a rapprochement between the senior Marxist and his one-time disciple, at odds since the latter part of 1903. Both detested "Liquidators," though Plekhanov favored persuasion rather than expulsion. Lenin now discovered that "Plekhanovism" was "the best product (and therefore the most vital) of the proletarian stream of Mensheviks."[6]

The "Vperyodists" transferred their school from Capri to Bologna in November, 1910. Trotsky joined Bogdanov, Lunacharsky, and lesser known Marxists as a lecturer, and perhaps as a demonstration of tolerance Lenin was again invited to participate. Predictably, he refused to be associated with such a tainted enterprise but repeated his offer to instruct the students in Paris.

Unable to undermine the Bologna school, he began one of his own in the village of Longjumeau near Paris in the spring of 1911.[7] The students, eighteen "regulars" and five auditors, were underground workers from Russia, including the inevitable police agent (except in this case there were two on hand). The faculty was quite distinguished—if political notoriety acquired later on is a proper criterion. Aside from Lenin, who lectured on political economy, the agrarian question, and the theory and practice of socialism, it included Zinoviev and Leo Kamenev, two aides who were to remain among the Bolshevik elite until purged in Stalin's Russia. Another instructor, Inessa Armand, maintained close ties with Lenin from 1910 until her death a decade later, and the nature of their relationship has given rise to a minor spasm of scholarly voyeurism in the West. Uncommonly attractive and vivacious for a female revolutionary—a type seldom noted for charm or physical beauty—she was a thirty-six-year old divorcee, the mother of five children, an accomplished linguist, and an excellent pianist. Lenin, though obviously fascinated by her, did not leave his wife. Speculation that they became lovers must remain unsatisfied in the absence of any conclusive evidence, which, if it exists, lies in the excessively puritanical hands of the Soviet authorities.[8]

Lenin returned to Paris late in August, 1911, and two weeks later attended a meeting of the International Socialist Bureau in Zurich, with intermediate stops for lectures and mountain climbing. After resuming his normal routine in Paris, his chief concern became the organization of a party conference that would vindicate the "correct" Leninist principles. Already, pursuing the strategy of previous occasions, he had sent emissaries to Russia to secure the necessary mandates from a constituency that was now largely illusory. But several were "Conciliators," sincerely interested in restoring party unity, and their leader, Alexei Rykov, was arrested shortly after his return. It developed that a police agent in Paris had informed on him in the expectation that "Conciliator" supporters in Russia would also be arrested, thus decreasing the chances for party unity. Gregory (Sergo) Ordzhonikidze, a Georgian Bolshevik more amenable to Lenin's wishes, was seemingly given a free hand by the Okhrana to pursue his mission. He established a committee in Russia that presumed to represent the party as a whole, and belated invitations to a conference in Prague were sent to all but the "Liquidators" (that is, the Menshevik majority led by Martov). Plekhanov and Trotsky, among others, refused to attend, well aware that Lenin's supporters would command an overwhelming majority and choke off any dissenting views.

Prior arrangements had been made with the Czech Social Democrats, whose People's House was placed at the disposal of the delegates as a meeting hall. Only fourteen had voting rights, and two of these turned out to be police agents. A lone Plekhanovite spoke out against Lenin's steamroller tactics, but there were few others who ventured to mar the near unanimity of the occasion by a critical word. The proceedings dragged on unconscionably (January 18–30, 1912) for so monolithic a gathering. Nothing momentous—or even memorable—was said, yet the Prague conference marked a significant departure in the history of Russian Social Democracy. Since 1905 Lenin had been obliged to give lip service to the concept of political unity, and now, by his bold attempt to substitute Bolshevism for the party he served notice that the split would no longer be disguised by paper compromises and semantic legerdemain. His new Central Committee (elected at Prague) consisted of six tested Leninists besides himself and included Zinoviev, Ordzhonikidze, and the most famous of the numerous police agents in Bolshevik ranks, Roman Malinovsky. Stalin, Lenin's Georgian protégé, was co-opted shortly afterward.

Ordinary party members in Russia, unskilled in émigré politics or fine points of doctrine, were confused by the whole affair. Many accepted Lenin's coup at face value, seeing in him the legitimate party leader despite outraged protests by his outflanked opponents. Trotsky took the initiative in rallying the anti-Leninists, although his original aim was one of reconciliation. But Lenin refused to be drawn into further unity efforts, and the so-called August Bloc came into being at a Social Democratic conference in Vienna during the summer of 1912. It was soon debilitated by factional quarrels, nor did it ever become clear whether its chief function was to combine against Lenin or to bind up the party's wounds.

The Bolsheviks reentered the field of legal party work in the spring of 1912 by publishing a daily newspaper in St. Petersburg. The name *Pravda* was appropriated—a dig at Trotsky, but also a concealed tribute because the Vienna *Pravda* had become the most popular of the underground papers smuggled into Russia, and its reputation would presumably rub off on the Bolshevik venture. Trotsky's shrill protests were in vain. Lenin advised the editor to reply: "It's a useless waste of time sending quarrelsome and complaining letters. They will not be answered."[9] The newspaper flourished and was instrumental in reviving the comatose Bolshevik organization in Russia. The government closed it down eight times in two years, and on each occasion the versatile editors changed its name and continued to publish. It was permanently banned in 1914 just before the war broke out. The rival Menshevik organ fell considerably short of *Pravda's* circulation but likewise helped to pump new life into the underground apparatus.

The Prague conference, followed by a revived strike movement in Russia during the spring, lifted Lenin's spirits and steadied his nerves. During the previous winter he had gloomily remarked to his sister Anna, then visiting in Paris, "I do not know whether I'll live to see the next rise of the tide."[10] In June, 1912, he and Krupskaya moved to Cracow, the historic Polish city then located in Austria-Hungary. Proximity to the Russian frontier, where he could maintain closer contacts with his agents and supervise *Pravda* and the Bolshevik delegation in the Duma, was probably the major reason for his change of residence. But the Okhrana, in collaboration with the French police, had become more than a nuisance, while the authorities in Cracow, mostly Polish, were anti-Russian. Now, at least, the mail would not be intercepted or tampered with. Lenin was pleased that there was "more literary work and less squabbling," but the library was poor and hard to reach. "However provincial and barbarous this town of ours may be," he informed his sister Maria, "on the whole I am better off here than I was in Paris."[11]

Elections to the Fourth Duma were held in the fall of 1912. The Social Democratic representation—six Bolsheviks and seven Mensheviks—continued to form a single "fraction" in response to the sentiment of its working-class constituency. Lenin demanded a split, but the logistics of enforcement were complicated and took months of preparation. He also discovered that *Pravda's* editors were a stubbornly independent lot. His contributions to the paper—they were to constitute an impressive total of about

270 items—were typically though not invariably acrimonious, and his tirades against the "Liquidators" were particularly abusive. That the editors dared soften or delete some of the more offensive passages (occasionally a whole article) infuriated him. He bombarded them with a series of letters that ran the emotional gamut from fiery indignation to querulous complaint, now and then dropping a word of commendation. The young editorial secretary, Vyacheslav Molotov, the future Soviet foreign minister, bore the brunt of his temper, though Lenin tactfully directed his correspondence to the "editor" or the "editorial board." Stalin was one of Molotov's superiors, and Lenin contrived to remove them both in a "reorganization" of the editorial staff early in 1913. He diplomatically summoned Stalin to Cracow for a conference with other members of the Central Committee and dispatched Jacob Sverdlov, a trusted and well-briefed aide, to the Russian capital for the necessary personnel changes. Not long afterward Sverdlov and Stalin were both arrested and deported to Siberia.

Malinovsky, the redoubtable *agent provocateur*, was responsible for the apprehension of his two colleagues. Recently elected to the Duma, he became the Bolshevik spokesman and vice-chairman of the Social Democratic delegation, and on Lenin's instructions he engineered the final break with the Menshevik deputies in the fall of 1913. His career as a double agent was often suspected, but since proof was lacking and most of the rumors emanated from Menshevik sources Lenin dismissed them as slanderous nonsense. In the spring of 1914 Malinovsky suddenly resigned from the Duma, citing "reasons of health," and sought out Lenin in Cracow. He claimed that the police had threatened to expose him as a convicted criminal—he did indeed have a prison record—but the actual reason was a shakeup in the Okhrana and a specific order by his new superiors to leave his Duma post. Lenin had misgivings, but accepted the story, and to forestall a Menshevik demand for a full party investigation he appointed one of his own that duly cleared Malinovsky. The damning police records were, inevitably, uncovered in 1917 after the fall of the monarchy. Lenin, though no doubt chagrined by his gullibility, professed to believe that the Bolsheviks had gained greater benefit from Malinovsky's services than the police, an unconvincing argument but not entirely without merit.

The final segment of the bizarre affair occurred in 1918 when Malinovsky returned voluntarily to Soviet Russia. He considered himself fully rehabilitated but was extraordinarily naive in supposing that Lenin would intercede on his behalf. He was tried, convicted, and shot. While the verdict was legally correct, there were, as Lenin tacitly admitted in 1917, extenuating circumstances. Although the term had not yet been invented or the condition diagnosed, Malinovsky, like others in the shadow world of the double agent, suffered from an "identity crisis" and was himself confused as to where his true loyalty lay. Subconsciously he sought to expiate his guilt by what would seem a foolhardy act in returning to the scene of his crimes.

In May, 1913, the Lenins, together with the Zinovievs and another Bolshevik couple, moved for the summer to the village of Poronin in the foothills of the Carpathians. Krupskaya suffered from a thyroid condition, and it was hoped that the bracing mountain air would prove therapeutic. But she became steadily worse, and in June Lenin took her to a specialist in Switzerland who performed an operation without the use of an anesthetic. Lenin lectured in several Swiss cities while she recovered. Her convalescence was cut short when Zinoviev telegraphed on urgent party business, and they hastened back to Poronin. Krupskaya, though improved, never fully regained her health.

In August, shortly after his return, Lenin held a strategy conference with the Central Committee. A somewhat larger Bolshevik meeting, including most of the Duma representatives, convened in October and decided to raise the question of another party congress, for Lenin remained unsatisfied with the clever but partial victory he had won at Prague. He and Krupskaya returned to Cracow for the winter months, as did Zinoviev, Kamenev, and Inessa Armand, who had recently been released from a tsarist prison. Lenin found the leisure to reread some of the Russian literary classics (Tolstoy's *Anna Karenina* for the "hundredth time") and even pored over a catalog of Moscow's Tretyakov Art Gallery. Krupskaya describes him in jest (but not inaccurately) as a "desperate nationalist." "You can't entice him to look at the works of Polish artists," she wrote her mother-in-law.[12]

The Mensheviks and their nominal allies condemned Lenin's arrogant split of the Social Democratic delegation in the Duma.

An appeal to the International Socialist Bureau for assistance brought an offer to mediate. Early in 1914 the Bureau's chairman, Emile Vandervelde of Belgium, journeyed to Russia for a personal investigation of the controversy. Lenin purported to welcome outside intervention and maintained that Bolshevik differences with the "Liquidators" were "the same as those between reformists and revolutionaries everywhere." Under the Bureau's good offices, a unity conference met in Brussels the following July. Lenin chose not to attend—he was "extremely nervous, almost ill"—and sent Inessa Armand, who knew French much better than he, to head the small Bolshevik contingent. She was to "convey to the enemy" only "our *conditions*," the "*objective facts*, and that's all!!'"[13] Lenin equipped her with an elaborate memorandum, most of which she read in a French translation to the assembled delegates. Plekhanov, who had been edging away from Lenin for some time, snorted indignantly that what purported to be terms for unity were "but articles of a new criminal code." As Lenin saw it, there was only one way to achieve unity—submission to Bolshevik leadership. His formal instructions to Armand put it more diplomatically but no less decisively: "Urge the minority, which has left the illegal party and is trying to confuse and disrupt its activities and the will of the majority, to abandon its practices and *prove in deed* that it is willing to respect the will of the majority."[14] The conference passed a unanimous resolution, with the abstention of four Leninists, calling for unity among the Russian Social Democrats and referring the dispute to the forthcoming congress of the Second International in Vienna. The meeting never took place: war, the first major European conflict in nearly a century, interposed an emphatic veto.

"A war between Austria and Russia would be useful for the revolution," Lenin had written Gorky early in 1913, "but it's not likely that Franz Joseph and Nicky will give us that pleasure."[15] His offhand remark turned out to be a vast understatement, not only as to the scope of the conflict but also its "usefulness" as a catalyst if not an incubator of revolutions. The venerable houses of Hohenzollern and Habsburg collapsed as ignominiously as but certainly less dramatically than that of the Romanovs, and the most outlandish event of all—the establishment of a Bolshevik regime in Russia—became a historical "accident" of staggering proportions and unforeseen duration.

Such political extrapolations were far from Lenin's mind in the summer of 1914. The Austrian declaration of war on Russia on August 6 automatically converted him into an enemy alien. A local policeman—the Lenins had returned to Poronin—searched the household, finding nothing more incriminating than an unloaded pistol and several notebooks containing suspicious-looking statistics on the agrarian question. Lenin was allowed to turn himself in the next day to the authorities at Novy Targ, the nearest town of any size. But he was not a hapless victim of circumstance and used the period of grace to good advantage. He wired the Cracow police, who knew him as a political exile, and enlisted the aid of Fürstenburg-Ganetsky, his well-connected colleague then in Poronin. Victor Adler, the leading Austrian Social Democrat, was alerted, and a number of other influential citizens interceded on his behalf. Nevertheless, he remained in jail eleven days and eventually received permission to leave for neutral Switzerland. The rail journey from Cracow to Vienna was slow and tedious, for military transport had priority. Not until September 5 did his party (it included Krupskaya and her mother) reach Berne, their final destination. At a stopover in Vienna he called on Adler and presumably tendered thanks for helping to secure his release. From Zurich he expressed his gratitude more formally in a letter whose warm salutation—"Esteemed Comrade!"—would seem wildly incongruous some months later when he was venting his anger at "social patriots" (of whom Adler was a prime example) supporting the war.

To Marxists it was axiomatic that industrial capitalism produced war, as it did the other evils of modern society. Many had half-convinced themselves that the class struggle had weaned the working class from national loyalties and that a major European conflict was therefore improbable if not impossible. Lenin never deluded himself to this extent, but he did expect that those who professed to speak in the name of the proletariat would remain faithful to their internationalist creed—that the Western socialists would denounce the war and that those holding parliamentary seats would vote against war credits. He was shocked and bitterly disillusioned when, with honorable excep-

tions, these supposed disciples of Marx betrayed their sacred
trust and joined the chauvinist frenzy. At first he refused to believe that the German Social Democrats had backed the Kaiser's
government, maintaining (in a bizarre example of wishful thinking) that an issue of their organ *Vorwärts* had been faked by the
"bourgeois German *canaille*." But the truth was apparent soon
enough, and he pronounced his verdict: "The Second International is dead, vanquished by opportunism."[16]

Judged by Leninist standards, the Russian Social Democrats
compiled the most creditable record of all the national parties.
Both Bolshevik and Menshevik deputies, after issuing a joint
declaration condemning the war, walked out of the Duma cham-
ber before the critical vote on the military budget. But the
Mensheviks soon showed signs of equivocation, while Lenin's
followers aggressively pursued a "defeatist" policy based on his
premise that the "lesser evil by far" in a war between Russia
and Germany would be the "defeat of the tsarist monarchy and
its army."[17] The Bolshevik representatives were arrested in November, 1914, despite their parliamentary immunity and placed
in solitary confinement. Together with Kamenev and other party
members, they were given a public trial and sentenced to exile
in Siberia. In his written comment on the affair, Lenin mildly
scolded the defendants for failing to set forth Bolshevik views
more forcefully and accused Kamenev of "incorrect" conduct
"from the standpoint of a revolutionary Social Democrat" (he
had been less than courageous in "neglecting" to denounce the
war effort). But their chief was obviously pleased that the court
proceedings had publicized the struggle against the war and
demonstrated that "the most progressive representatives of the
proletariat in Russia" were "hostile to chauvinism."[18]

Among low-level Social Democrats there were numerous defec-
tions from the party organization, though many were merely
patriotic backsliders who returned to the fold once the wartime
hysteria had died away. Among the prominent Marxist émigrés,
Plekhanov was one of the few who became an avowed patriot.
Lenin found it difficult to comprehend how the man he still
greatly respected despite their past quarrels could stoop so low
as to become a hated "defensist." He made a point of attending
Plekhanov's address at Lausanne in October, 1914. Given ten
minutes for a rebuttal, he spoke with outward serenity, but the

pallor of his face betrayed great agitation. Plekhanov had the last word, and his witty rebuttal won enthusiastic applause from the Menshevik sympathizers who dominated the audience. It was to be the last personal confrontation between the patriarch of Russian socialism and his former pupil, the one reduced to political impotence and the other on the threshold of world fame.

Lenin's position on the war had nothing in common with pacifism, an attitude that had penetrated certain segments of reformist socialism in the West. His major slogan—"Turn the imperialist war into a civil war"—represented the epitome of revolutionary extremism but had no practical application until war weariness began to erode the patriotic resolve of public opinion. In Russia, where casualties were higher and the government more inept than in the other belligerent countries, that process was accelerated to such an extent that by 1915 defeatism (or at least apathy toward the war) had begun to infect the working masses. But Bolshevik propaganda was scarcely responsible for this decay of civilian morale, and only a tiny minority shared Lenin's view that a German victory over Russia, while not in itself desirable, would help the cause of European revolution by insuring the collapse of tsarist absolutism.

Lenin's wartime contacts with the Russian underground were necessarily of the most tenuous sort. His key link, Alexander Shlyapnikov, maintained headquarters in Stockholm and smuggled illegal literature into Russia via Finland. Their correspondence was filled with Lenin's reproaches and complaints, yet he was often solicitous about his hard-working assistant and even, on occasion, apologetic. "You can't . . . be nervous and fall into despair," he chided in a letter written in May, 1916. "Indeed, that's not the proletarian way . . . chiefs have no right to have attacks of nerves!!"[19] (A psychologist might conclude that subconsciously he was as concerned about his own periods of despondency and "nerves" as he was with Shlyapnikov's.)

Many of Lenin's potential allies, both Russian émigrés and Western socialists, tended to shy away from the provocative militancy of his wartime stand. They preferred to call for a general peace without annexations or indemnities as a more realistic method of rallying the majority socialists and ending the war. In short, they sought compromise, just as the Mensheviks had vainly pursued negotiations with the Bolsheviks for the sake of unity in a common struggle. But as a matter of temperament as well as principle Lenin spurned the moderates, though sparing them the abuse that he reserved for the "traitors." In September, 1915, however, at the tiny Swiss village of Zimmerwald near Berne, he participated in a conference with other European socialists who opposed the war, including Trotsky and Martov. The assembled delegates—thirty-eight from eleven different countries—agreed on a manifesto that Lenin considered timid and inconsistent but nevertheless an incipient break with "opportunism and social-chauvinism." His point of view, as a French delegate put it, was "dominated not by the desire for peace but by the wish to erect the foundation pillars of a new International. This is what divides us. We want a manifesto which promotes peace; we don't want to emphasize what divides us but what unites us."[20] Neither the manifesto nor the proceedings of the conference aroused much attention beyond a narrow circle of sympathetic left-wingers, but hostile comment did emanate from the organs controlled by the majority socialists.

The so-called Zimmerwald Left, a small group of "internationalists" headed by Lenin and Zinoviev, continued to agitate for a stronger policy statement. They were partially successful in pushing through a more revolutionary appeal to the European masses at a second and slightly larger conference held in April, 1916, at Kienthal, another picturesque Swiss village. While avoiding Lenin's bold "civil war" formula, it called for the "seizure of political power and the abolition of capitalist property by the working class" as the "one effective means of preventing future wars."[21] The meetings at Zimmerwald and Kienthal were seemingly little more than a defiant and rather futile gesture, for even the "moderates" were isolated and presumably discredited minorities in their own national parties. Yet with more chronological perspective (and increasing disillusionment with the war), the Zimmerwaldists appeared to better advantage as socialism's "better conscience." Latent guilt feelings stirred among the majority socialists, and the later success of Lenin's Third International in splitting the demoralized ranks of European socialism was not unrelated to the obscure ideological currents set in motion at Zimmerwald and Kienthal.

Lenin moved to Zurich in February, 1916. The "petty bourgeois dullness" of life in Berne furnished a possible motive, but
his decision was largely pragmatic: the superior library resources
of Zurich. He was already hard at work researching the topic of
imperialism and borrowed freely from John A. Hobson's *Imperialism* (1906), a seminal but distinctly non-Marxist critique
by the British economist and social critic, and from Rudolf
Hilferding's *Finance Capital* (1910), the scholarly work of an
Austrian Marxist. Lenin's brochure, intended for legal publication under the tsarist censorship (thus containing some "accursed
Aesopian language"), was delayed and appeared in 1917 under
the title *Imperialism, the Highest Stage of Capitalism* after his
return to Russia. "Menshevik elements" in the publishing firm
allegedly deleted passages criticizing Martov and Kautsky and
"made corrections in the manuscript that not only destroyed the
originality of Lenin's style but also distorted his ideas."[22] Both
Lenin and Hobson condemned imperialism, but the latter was
more concerned to demonstrate its immorality than to attack
the economic system that made it possible. Lenin reversed the
order, arguing that imperialism was inevitable when the stage
of monopoly capitalism had been reached. Having exhausted
their domestic markets, the capitalists, in their insatiable greed
for profits, found in colonial and semi-colonial countries a ready
source of raw materials and cheap labor, an outlet for invest-
ment capital, and a previously untapped market for finished
products. The embarrassing failure of orthodox Marxists to
account for the growing prosperity of the proletariat (they were
supposed to be increasingly miserable) was explained with simple
but convincing ingenuity. The Western worker was, in effect,
being granted a bonus through the ruthless exploitation of the
colonial masses. As Lenin added in a special preface in 1920,
it was from these "enormous super-profits" (beyond the normal
amount squeezed from the working class) that bribes were provided for labor leaders and the "aristocracy of labor." Lenin
could thus explain in one neat formula why the "contradictions"
of capitalism had not led to social revolution and why "reformism
and chauvinism" permeated the ranks of socialism. Whatever its
flaws as an updating of Marxism, Lenin's thesis was to have an
incalculable global impact—and not solely upon doctrinaire socialists. For its timing was precisely right: the war itself, dragging

on interminably, seemed a classic example of imperialism in action, an "inevitable" result of the decadence of monopoly capitalism.

But Lenin was not content to make his mark as an isolated theoretician. Scholarship to him was but a tool to serve higher political ends. In July, 1916, when he completed his manuscript, there were no hints that revolution, either in Russia or abroad, was imminent.

CHAPTER VI

The Bolshevik Revolution

LENIN'S RECEPTION UPON HIS ARRIVAL IN PETROGRAD ON APRIL 16, 1917, was lavish and hospitable. His views were known to be "radical," but the "revolutionary democracy" was tolerant of dissent (except for tsarist supporters), and he was welcomed back to "free Russia" with the enthusiasm befitting a distinguished Marxist who had dedicated his life to the revolutionary cause. Rank and file Bolsheviks, workers' delegations, soldiers from the local garrison, and sailors from the nearby naval base at Kronstadt formed the core of greeters, while a guard of honor, a military band, and the Menshevik leaders of the Petrograd Soviet conferred a more official flavor upon the reception. Someone thrust a large bouquet into Lenin's hands, and Shlyapnikov, acting as master of ceremonies, escorted him to a waiting room formerly reserved for the royal family.

The chairman of the Soviet, Nikolai Chkheidze, delivered a brief but homiletic speech of welcome, suggesting that Lenin would do well to close ranks and defend the revolution from its enemies, both foreign and domestic. Casually ignoring him, Lenin addressed the crowd as the "vanguard of the international proletarian army." "The hour is not far distant," he declared, "when . . . the people will turn their weapons against the capitalist exploiters. . . . Germany is seething. . . . Any day now the whole of European imperialism may collapse. The Russian Revolution you have achieved has prepared the way and opened a new epoch. Long live the worldwide socialist revolution!"[1]

Lenin and his party left the station by the main entrance. He was led to an automobile, but the crowd outside insisted on a speech, and he obligingly climbed on the hood for a brief recapitulation of his earlier remarks. Then, in an armored car and accompanied by the band, his Bolshevik escort, and a milling throng, he made his way in a slow procession to the Kshesinskaya mansion (owned by a ballerina, once a favorite of the deposed Tsar before his marriage, and commandeered by the Bolsheviks as party headquarters). At nearly every intersection he paused to say a few words, varying his message only slightly.

Once at their destination, Lenin and his entourage were provided with tea and snacks. He endured a tedious round of ceremonial oratory and finally rose to his feet, apparently to acknowledge the reception that his hosts had so thoughtfully provided. But with the instinct of the true political animal he launched into a ninety-minute address upbraiding his lieutenants for collaborating with the bourgeois Provisional Government and sounding the opening note in a campaign for a *socialist* revolution in Russia. Stunned, his devoted disciples applauded enthusiastically while striving to adjust themselves to their leader's topsy-turvy Marxism. Whether Bolshevik or Menshevik, the Social Democrats had absorbed as a matter of course the fundamental dictum that socialism was possible only when capitalism had properly matured, when the bourgeois social order had reached the correct stage in the historical process. Now they were being told that their backward land, barely rid of the dragging anchor of tsarism, could somehow serve as a staging area for a European socialist revolution (Lenin was careful to avoid saying that socialism was immediately feasible in Russia, though this subtle distinction was probably lost on most of his audience).

Dawn was breaking when Lenin, who must have been exhausted by this time, left for his sister Anna's apartment. He and Krupskaya shared a separate room, their residence until early July. After a few hours of rest—Lenin always managed with amazingly little sleep when working under pressure—he conferred with colleagues, visited the offices of *Pravda,* and even found time to pay filial respects at his mother's grave (she had died less than a year before). In the afternoon he attended a Social Democratic conference at the Tauride Palace, where the Duma, now virtually defunct, had met since 1906.

The organizers of the meeting hoped to reunite the splintered party, a goal that seemed to have a better chance of success in the friendly environment of revolutionary Petrograd than in the strained atmosphere of émigré politics. But Lenin neatly sabotaged the apostles of unity by repeating to a largely hostile audience the gist of what he had told his followers earlier that day.

Published in *Pravda* and known thereafter as the April Theses, his "report on the tasks of the revolutionary proletariat" was a sweeping repudiation of the political honeymoon that all factions of the Center and Left had enjoyed since the overthrow of the Tsar. He called for withdrawal of all support to the Provisional Government and a transfer of state power to the Soviet of Workers' Deputies, where Bolshevik representation, though still very weak, had every prospect of improvement. He repeated his denunciation of the "imperialist war" but expediently avoided a plea for peace negotiations in view of the still overwhelming "defensist" sentiment. As for the land question, estates should be confiscated and all land nationalized, its disposition to be determined by local Soviets of peasants and agricultural laborers. To preserve Bolshevism from contamination by the socialist patriots, the party should abandon its Social Democratic affiliation by forthrightly accepting the name "Communist" and proceed to the establishment of a new organization to replace the discredited Second International.

Lenin's opponents thought his program fantastic and, unlike his bewildered but respectful adherents, were not slow to say so. A Menshevik, Boris Bogdanov (not to be confused with the "Machist" Bogdanov), pronounced it the "raving of a madman," and Joseph Goldenberg, once Lenin's faithful lieutenant, accused him of planting the "banner of civil war in the midst of revolutionary democracy" and preaching the "superannuated truths of primitive anarchism." He had made himself a "candidate for one European throne that has been vacant for thirty years—the throne of Bakunin!"[2] A more charitable judgment held that Lenin was simply out of touch with Russian realities and would reject his own "abstract constructions" when given time to reorient himself.

Despite his unquestioned moral authority as the founder and leader of Bolshevism, Lenin was in no position to dominate his party by mere fiat. *Pravda,* reflecting the views of Kamenev, spoke for the majority when on April 8 it declared his program "unacceptable because it begins from the assumption that the bourgeois democratic revolution has ended." It was indeed a sharp break with Marxism as Lenin himself had perceived it. Yet within two weeks his superior skills as a debater and lobbyist, together with pressure from the rank and file, proved decisive. His "official" victory, delayed until the all-Russian Bolshevik conference in May, was strengthened by the Provisional Government's blundering conduct of foreign policy.

Paul Milyukov, the Kadet leader and minister of foreign affairs, was a poorly disguised imperialist, so anxious for Russia to acquire the historic straits of the Bosporus and Dardanelles that his presence in the cabinet lent credence to Lenin's strictures about "predatory capitalist governments." The Soviet desire for a "peace without annexations or indemnities" and the "self-determination of peoples" was transmitted on May 1 to the Allied powers after sufficient pressure had been exerted upon the Provisional Government. But Milyukov succeeded in adding an "explanation" that robbed the Soviet formula of substance, and when the text became known serious anti-government demonstrations broke out. The more militant workers and soldiers took the Bolshevik slogan, "All power to the Soviets," quite literally, while the Mensheviks and Socialist Revolutionaries dominating the Soviet Executive Committee sought only a veto right without the responsibility of political authority.

The government survived on the sufferance of the Soviet. Another "explanation" was published (though never sent to the Allies as promised) and the cabinet reorganized. Milyukov was dropped, the "radical" lawyer Alexander Kerensky (a Trudovik and nominal socialist) shifted to the War Ministry and five socialists joined the government to dilute its "capitalist" flavor. Lenin could take grim satisfaction from the government's first crisis, for his diagnosis of the "imperialist war" had evoked a mass response sooner than expected. Ironically, he was placed in the position of restraining the "ultras" in the party who had supported the demonstrators' slogan, "Down with the Provisional Government!" He wanted only a "peaceful reconnaissance of the enemy's strength, not to give battle," and a resolution of the Central Committee condemned "attempts of an adventurist character."

To Lenin the essence of revolutionary strategy was proper timing, and he admitted that the party had shown signs of disorganization and vacillation during the May events. But a premature attack on state power might lead to disaster. "The Provisional Government must be overthrown," he told the party leaders on May 7, "but not now and not in the usual way."

The war fever, notwithstanding Milyukov's unfortunate experience, had abated only slightly. "To be a socialist while chauvinism is the craze is to be in the minority." The peasants, though land hungry and growing impatient, remained patriotic and temporarily beyond the reach of Bolshevik propaganda. "If we want to draw the peasantry into the revolution," Lenin concluded, "we must keep the proletarian apart from it in a . . . separate party, for the peasantry is chauvinistic. To attract the *muzhik* now means surrendering to the mercies of Milyukov."[3]

Bolshevik ranks swelled with new recruits during the spring, more than offsetting the resignation of a small minority who disagreed with the Leninist dispensation. There was, however, a serious gap in leadership between Lenin himself and his principal assistants. Kamenev and Stalin had been reluctantly won over; Zinoviev was a useful agitator, Sverdlov a good organizer, and Bukharin an able theoretician. But a prestige figure of Lenin's stature was sorely lacking, and the belated arrival of Trotsky (who had been detained in Canada on his journey from New York) provided the Bolsheviks with a superb "mob orator" and a writer of rare distinction. Lenin, in contrast, was seldom at ease with a mass audience, nor was his literary style a model of grace and elegance. During the war Trotsky's views had gradually converged with those of Lenin, and he decided to cast his lot with the Bolsheviks when he sensed the revolutionary possibilities that lay ahead. Considering their personality differences— and the venomous remarks they had exchanged in the heat of ideological combat—the two worked together with unusual harmony and mutual understanding. Trotsky delayed his formal allegiance to the party until August, for his pride and independence did not permit a sudden capitulation to a disciplined organization still somewhat alien to his temperament. His small following—"a pleiade of brillant generals without an army"— also had to be placated. Most of them became converts and added considerable luster to the party, though none, with the possible exception of Lunacharsky, achieved political prominence in 1917.

At the First Congress of Soviets, which opened in Petrograd on June 16, the Bolshevik delegation of 105 was lost among the 1,090 representatives, some with no formal party affiliation or voting rights. Yet there were already unmistakable signs that the

Bolshevik message had received the approval of a substantial majority of the workers in the capital and had made solid inroads in Moscow and other industrial centers. The villages remained largely indifferent, for the peasants were traditionally loyal to the Socialist Revolutionaries insofar as they responded to party doctrine. Already the "dark people" were resorting to violence in the provinces south of Moscow and in the region of the middle Volga. (Lenin opposed "anarchist seizures" but favored a peaceful transfer of the land to the peasants.) The soldiers, largely peasants in uniform, acquired a more rapid political education under the stress of a losing war. Many "voted with their feet" and deserted, hastening back to their villages for a share of the land. But the army retained its cohesion and a semblance of discipline, largely because the Germans, for sensible political reasons, refrained from conducting an offensive. The Petrograd garrison, untypical of the army as a whole, was thoroughly "radicalized" by midsummer and went over to the Bolsheviks in increasing numbers.

If the Executive Committee of the Petrograd Soviet, with some ninety members, was too unwieldy to transact much business, the Congress of Soviets could only become a semi-public forum. Lenin made a brief address, arousing laughter and ironic applause when he referred to the assertion of Irakli Tsereteli, a Menshevik cabinet minister, that no party was ready to assume political power: "There is! No party can refuse it, and our party certainly doesn't; we are ready to take full power at any moment."[4] Most of the delegates still regarded the Bolsheviks as deluded fanatics, unaware that they were no longer the isolated sectarians of two months before. Lenin, despite his bold words, was unprepared for an armed seizure of power, nor did he contemplate abandoning support of the Soviets, at least as a tactical slogan. But he was certainly not averse to taking power by peaceful means and clearly foresaw that the Soviet organization furnished a "legal" and quite logical method of displacing the Provisional Government.

As a show of strength while the congress was still in session, the Bolsheviks planned a mass demonstration for June 23. A few hotheads suggested more vigorous action but were overruled. The leaders of the Petrograd Soviet, recalling the disorders in early May and fearing a coup d'état, announced a ban on all demonstrations for three days, and the Soviet Congress endorsed the decision. The Bolsheviks were faced with a dilemma: ignominiously to abandon their plans at the risk of alienating their zealous followers or to defy the Soviet decree in contradiction to their insistent demand that political power should reside with the Soviet organization. At the last minute Lenin (backed by the Central Committee) chose to call off the demonstration, barely leaving time for the compositors at *Pravda* to substitute a counter-proclamation.

Bolshevik agitators joined emissaries from the Soviet Congress in the factories and the barracks in an attempt to justify the cancellation order and to forestall any impromptu protests. Their reception, particularly of the Soviet speakers, was often rude and even hostile, but the streets of the capital remained quiet. Lenin grumbled in *Pravda* that "an ordinary bourgeois government can ban demonstrations only on constitutional grounds and after declaring martial law," while "an extraordinary and near-socialist government can ban demonstrations without any grounds and on the strength of 'facts' known only to itself."[5]

The Bolshevik setback, though embarrassing, was temporary. The Soviet leadership, unwilling to concede that the popularity of the Menshevik-Socialist Revolutionary majority had eroded, authorized a giant procession on July 1 that would constitute a vote of confidence. But instead of the innocuous slogans recommended by the Soviet—"Universal Peace," "A Democratic Republic," etc.—the marchers, some 400,000 strong, indicated a decided preference for banners with the Bolshevik watchwords: "Down with the Ten Minister-Capitalists!," "Bread-Peace-Freedom," and—not yet abandoned—"All Power to the Soviets!" Lenin, who had taken a personal interest in preparing the placards and banners, exulted in *Pravda* that within a few hours the demonstration had dissipated, "like a handful of dust, the empty talk about Bolshevik conspirators and showed with the utmost clarity that the vanguard of the toiling masses of Russia, the industrial proletariat of the capital, and the overwhelming majority of the troops stand behind the slogans that our party has always advocated."[6]

The Soviet fiasco in Petrograd was matched by a far more serious fiasco for the Provisional Government on the Austrian front. War Minister Kerensky, displaying commendable energy and an impressive but frenzied eloquence, had for several weeks harangued the troops on their sacred duty to defend the revolution by carrying the offensive to the enemy. The ill-conceived enterprise, designed principally to bolster Russia's "honor" among its allies and to revive the government's sagging prestige, began on July 1 and ended in a disastrous rout as German and Austro-Hungarian units counterattacked in force.

Russia's military collapse, a shattering blow to the dwindling number of patriots, confirmed the steady disintegration of the armed forces. It was a situation made to order for the Bolsheviks, whose "subversion," so bitterly resented by the moderate socialists as well as the "bourgeoisie," had penetrated well beyond the Petrograd garrison. Yet they were the beneficiaries, not the initiators, of the debacle, and however insidious their propaganda, it would have made little impact upon an army whose morale had not already been undermined by three years of a sanguinary and futile conflict.

The ill-fated July offensive added fuel to the seething resentment of the workers and soldiers in the capital, who had far outstripped the rest of the country in revolutionary fervor. Lenin perceived as early as the abortive June demonstration the near impossibility of reconciling his political commitments: finding a satisfactory outlet for the tempestuous but fickle Bolshevik clientele while striving to avoid a premature insurrection that could lead only to disaster. His ingenuity was taxed to the limit when on July 16 the First Machine Gun Regiment poured into the streets, the leading echelon in a vast popular outburst that he later described as "something considerably more than a demonstration and less than a revolution."

Lenin, whose recurrent malady—headaches and insomnia—still troubled him, was enjoying a badly needed rest in Finland at the country home of Vladimir Bonch-Bruyevich, an old party associate. The Bolshevik Central Committee, divided and hesitant, dispatched a messenger, and he rushed back to Petrograd on the morning of July 17. Armed soldiers and workers, joined by some 20,000 turbulent sailors from Kronstadt, were out in force and in no mood for compromise. A crowd gathered at the Kshesinskaya mansion, where Lenin had gone from the railway station. At first declining to speak because of illness, he finally came out on the balcony and received a rousing ovation. But his brief remarks were subdued, and his concluding appeal for self-restraint and vigilance was disappointing, especially to the belligerent Kronstadt sailors.

The Bolshevik leaders, by temporizing and waiting on events, lost their tenuous hold on the masses. A huge crowd gathered in front of the Tauride Palace, and its mood was ugly after mysterious gunfire from "provocateurs" along the route of the march had caused sudden panic, itchy trigger fingers, and not a few casualties. With proper organization and leadership the soldiers, sailors, and workers could have taken power in short order. But Lenin recognized the long odds against extending a Bolshevik success to the provinces, and if he contemplated an immediate coup, as his enemies charged, he was strangely diffident about the necessary measures to implement it. While the government's weakness may have tempted him to fill the yawning power vacuum in the name of the Soviet, the available evidence indicates no serious attempt—or even a contingency plan—by the Bolshevik general staff to encourage or to coordinate the armed strength that was temporarily theirs to command.

By late evening the aimless violence and pent-up rage of the street crowds had spent itself. Regiments previously disposed toward neutrality marched to the Tauride Palace to offer their services to the Soviet. These belated "loyalists" were motivated in part by data that the Ministry of Justice released with premature haste supposedly proving that Lenin and his henchmen were German agents. Such accusations had long been a staple of the right-wing press but were now buttressed by "documentation" which, though flimsy and unpersuasive, was seemingly authenticated by its "official" origin.[7] The substance of the charge, that German money was being indirectly funneled to the Bolsheviks, was probably accurate but could hardly be confirmed by the available evidence. In any case, public opinion was in a highly volatile mood and turned sharply against the Bolsheviks, permitting a show of force by the hitherto sluggish Provisional Government.

On July 18 Petrograd was delivered up to a "counterrevolutionary orgy" in which military detachments and "patriotic" vigilantes roamed the streets seeking vengeance. Soldiers seized and wrecked the offices of *Pravda* and its printing presses, just missing Lenin, who had departed for the first of a series of local hideouts. The Kshesinskaya mansion was also secured and warrants issued for the arrest of Lenin, Zinoviev, Kamenev, and other leading Bolsheviks. Trotsky, with characteristic bravado, demanded that he be placed on the same footing, although he was not yet a party member and, as a prominent Menshevik observed ironically, he forgot to leave his address. At first Lenin argued that he ought to make a court appearance, but his colleagues persuaded him that there was a possibility of a "legal lynching"— or to use the classic formula of quasi-official assassins, that he might be "shot while trying to escape."

Late in the evening of July 24, after staying several days in the apartment of Sergei Alliluyev, a friend of Stalin's, Lenin and Zinoviev slipped out of Petrograd by train. Their guide, Nikolai Yemelyanov, arranged temporary accommodations for them in a hayloft adjoining his cottage near Razliv, a village outside the city. A few days later they moved to a more isolated spot on the shore of a nearby lake and lived in a hut built of branches and thatched with hay. A cleared space in a dense thicket became Lenin's "green office," as he called it, and a log served as a makeshift desk. Yemelyanov's wife and sons provided the two with food and newspapers, while party couriers shuttled back and forth from Petrograd with a frequency and discretion sufficient to maintain Lenin's contact with what remained of the Central Committee (Kamenev and Trotsky, among others, were jailed but eventually released). He produced his usual articles for the Bolshevik press: *Pravda*'s demise did not prevent its perpetuation, as in tsarist times, under pseudonymous disguises. But his chief literary work during his enforced isolation was a theoretical essay published in 1918 as *State and Revolution*.

Lenin's pamphlet, widely known in the West but somewhat neglected in the Soviet Union because of its embarrassing strain of utopian anarchism, had its genesis in Zurich during the winter of 1916–17. His preliminary manuscript bore the working title of "Marxism on the State." Since the final version reveals no basic alterations in his theory of the state, it cannot be considered (as it has been by most Western scholars) merely an aberrant product of his "revolutionary fever" in 1917, an inexplicable departure from the Leninist canon. But it does present a startling contrast between theory and practice, for the celebrated Marxist dictum concerning the "withering away of the state" is accepted uncritically, and in Lenin's lifetime (not to mention that of his successor) the power and function of the Soviet state expanded to a degree undreamed of under the Tsars. Nor does he remark more than superficially upon the role of the party, the distinctive feature of *What Is to Be Done?* and his lesser political writings. His vision of the socialist future is curiously simplistic—in the light of what was to transpire—and his premises about human nature seem remarkably naive even by the unsophisticated standards of 1917 when psychology was in some respects still a backward stepchild of philosophy. The abolition of capitalism, he maintains, will work a profound transformation upon society and in time eliminate greed and self-interest so that people will "voluntarily work *according to their ability*" and "take freely" according to their needs. The evils of capitalist bureaucracy can be avoided by equality of income and supervision of society's business, "which any literate person can perform," by appropriate measures of "registration, filing, and checking." Although Lenin provided no timetables and was deliberately utopian in his approach, *State and Revolution* must necessarily receive low marks when judged by a later and more cynical generation.[8]

Kerensky assumed the premiership on July 21, but the negotiations to assemble another coalition cabinet took over two weeks, and the resulting Government of National Salvation inspired little confidence in the public at large. It had, in the words of a self-described "trouble-shooter and pen-pusher" for the Soviet Executive Committee, "no strength, no vision, no courage, and no prestige."[9] The massive unrest that had culminated in the July Days was temporarily stilled. The Bolsheviks licked their wounds, content for the moment to pursue a semi-clandestine existence. The pressure for instant—or even long-range—solutions to major problems having eased, Kerensky pursued the path of least resistance and continued to defer basic questions to the authority of a future Constituent Assembly.

The Bolshevik slogan calling for the transfer of state power to the Soviets was now obsolete. Under their Socialist Revolutionary and Menshevik leadership, Lenin wrote in late July, the Soviets were "like sheep led to the slaughterhouse and bleating pitifully under the knife" of the triumphant counterrevolution. "Only the revolutionary workers, if supported by the peasant poor, are capable of breaking the resistance of the capitalists and leading the people to take over the land without compensation, complete freedom, victory over famine and the war, and a just and lasting peace."[10]

Had he been completely candid, Lenin might have added that without Bolshevik guidance and direction the revolutionary workers and poor peasants, alone and unaided, were incapable of achieving these ambitious goals. If the party had been knocked out of combat for the time being, he was confident that it would reemerge stronger and more purposeful than ever. The convalescent recovered so rapidly that by the second week in August a Bolshevik congress of 267 delegates convened in Petrograd, somewhat furtively perhaps, but claiming to represent 240,000 members (an obvious exaggeration but according to the party bookkeepers a trebled increase in a little over three months). In Lenin's absence—he was unanimously elected honorary chairman—Sverdlov presided while Stalin and Bukharin delivered the principal reports. The chief debate centered on Lenin's revised strategy, and despite the reluctance of some delegates to abandon the Soviets and of others to endorse the view that Russia was ready for a socialist revolution, the key resolution passed with no dissenting votes and only four abstentions. Although the party was not specifically designated as the organ that would replace the Soviets on the assumption of state power, it was implicitly understood that the "revolutionary masses" could not spontaneously accomplish such a feat.

On August 25, nine days after the Bolshevik congress dissolved, the Moscow State Conference met at the Bolshoi Theater in an attempt to rally support for the Provisional Government and solidify national unity. An improvised substitute for a meaningful legislative body (or the long-promised Constituent Assembly), it purported to gather the "living forces of the country" under a single roof. The 2,414 delegates represented virtually every national organization except the Bolsheviks, who promptly denounced the meeting as counterrevolutionary, refused to attend a single session, and called an effective strike of Moscow workers on the opening day. The attempt to balance the organized forces of conservatism and liberalism grossly discriminated against the unaffiliated masses, for no effort was made to seat delegates on the basis of proportional representation. Yet it scarcely mattered, for the high-flown rhetoric, reaching a new pitch of irrelevant hysteria with Kerensky's speech on the closing day, marked a singularly futile episode in the unhappy chronicle of the Provisional Government.

The Moscow assembly exposed a new personality to the public gaze in General Lavr Kornilov, the army's recently appointed commander-in-chief. A symbolic man of destiny to his conservative admirers, he was almost a perfect stereotype of the honest soldier: personally courageous, intensely patriotic, and politically illiterate. The Bolsheviks had employed the word "counter-revolution" with such loose abandon after the July Days that it was already corrupted by misuse when a real counterrevolutionary danger arose. Even Kerensky, a most unsuitable candidate for the role of dictator, had been tarred by Lenin with the Bonapartist label. And Trotsky, never at a loss for a ringing phrase, had declared him the "mathematical center of Russian Bonapartism." The premier awoke rather late to the realization that Kornilov, a useful knight to slay the Bolshevik dragon, was either unprepared to make a distinction among the various brands of socialism or unaware that any existed. In his view, Kerensky, too, was a socialist of sorts and slated for political oblivion, if not something more sinister.

The Petrograd Soviet, taking upon itself the defense of the capital, invited the Bolsheviks to participate, and they responded with alacrity, reviving the Red Guard (workers' militia) that had been largely disbanded after the July Days. But military preparations proved superfluous. The railroad workers sabotaged Kornilov's troop movements, and Soviet agitators (mostly Bolsheviks) swarmed among his men. By September 12, without a shot being fired, the counterrevolutionary threat collapsed, and the attacking army demobilized itself as rapidly as that dispatched the previous March to take Petrograd for the Tsar. Kornilov and his leading officers were placed under token arrest, and most of them later fought the Bolsheviks in the civil war.

The Kornilov affair provided an instant tonic to the Bolshevik cause, still somewhat anemic in the absence of Lenin and his chief aides. "An adventure of a small group," Kerensky lamented, "was transformed in the inflamed imagination of the masses to a conspiracy of the whole of the bourgeoisie and of all the upper classes."[11] Whatever the state of their imagination, the workers and soldiers were seething with anger and resentment. The faint-hearted who had deserted the Bolsheviks in July returned, while others, disillusioned with the moderate socialists, joined the party or gave it moral support. This sudden access of strength was recorded in the Petrograd Soviet on September 13 and in the Moscow Soviet five days later when Bolshevik majorities were returned for the first time.

Early in September Lenin had left his hiding place near Petrograd for a safer haven in Finland. Clean shaven, wearing a wig, and provided with false identity papers, he crossed the border in a wood-burning locomotive disguised as a fireman and played his role to the hilt by energetically throwing logs into the firebox. He stayed for a time in Helsingfors (Helsinki) at the home of a Finnish Social Democrat who was also the acting police chief, certainly the ideal hideout for a fugitive. At the end of the month he moved to Vyborg because of its proximity to Petrograd and the Central Committee, finding lodgings with a staff member of a local labor newspaper. By this time he judged that the revolutionary crisis had matured. He had already begun the long and arduous task of persuading his reluctant subordinates that an armed uprising was feasible: "History will not forgive us," he argued, "if we do not take power now."[12]

The Provisional Government, which had always relied upon the Soviet for whatever authority it possessed, lost even that claim to legitimacy. The Mensheviks, whose membership had declined drastically, and the Socialist Revolutionaries, split into three factions, no longer provided Kerensky with any sizable base of mass support. His government, again reorganized on October 7, continued to function only because no one except Lenin was prepared to bring it down. Had the Bolsheviks not been driven to deliver the coup de grace by their leader, it seems likely that anarchism or military rule on a provincial scale would have succeeded Kerensky's floundering "revolutionary democracy."

Briefly, in mid-September, Lenin had toyed with the idea of collaborating with the moderate socialists to achieve a "dictatorship of the revolutionary proletariat." But he made no formal overture and, as the "popular front" atmosphere dissipated following Kornilov's abortive putsch, he quickly changed his mind. He dismissed the Democratic Conference, a popular consultative assembly (essentially a Menshevik-Socialist Revolutionary contrivance) that began meeting in Petrograd on September 27, as representing "only the compromising upper strata of the petty bourgeoisie." The Bolsheviks sent a grass-roots delegation of sixty-six, and their rowdy conduct contrasted sharply with the wordy gentility of the intelligentsia that largely dominated the conference. Lenin demanded a boycott: "You will be traitors and blockheads if you don't send the whole Bolshevik faction back to the factories and workshops, surround the Democratic Conference and arrest all those scoundrels."[13] The members of the Central Committee, reports Bukharin, gasped in astonishment and in lieu of more constructive action decided to burn the letter (but prudently, it seems, retaining a copy for the party archives).

Lenin lost the argument with his colleagues over the Democratic Conference. When it finally ended his unusual benediction, "Thank God, one more farce is behind us," was premature. For the conference melted into the Council of the Republic (popularly known as the Pre-Parliament) and resumed its deliberations, determined to remain at least a debating forum until the Constituent Assembly met. Again the question of Bolshevik participation arose, and the boycotters won a narrow majority in the Central Committee, only to be overruled at a party conference. Trotsky, released from prison on bail and recently chosen president of the Petrograd Soviet, led the party delegation at the first session on October 20. After a ringing speech, whose contents were already familiar to Bolshevik watchers, he staged a demonstrative walkout of his followers. The abrupt withdrawal had the look of spontaneity but was prearranged at a party caucus.

Lenin had been growing increasingly restive and irritated in Vyborg. His protracted absence from the party command post impaired his authority, and a series of stinging communiqués and waspish comments had not achieved the desired result in lighting a fire under his overly cautious lieutenants. Exasperated, he fired off a virtual ultimatum on October 12: "Seeing that the Central Committee has *even left unanswered* my urgent demands for such a policy [of seizing power] ever since the beginning of the Democratic Conference, that the central organ is *deleting* from my articles all references to such glaring errors . . . as the shameful decision to participate in the Pre-Parliament, the admission of Mensheviks to the Presidium of the Soviet, etc., etc.—

seeing this, I must regard it as a 'subtle' hint at the unwillingness of the Central Committee even to consider the question, a subtle hint that I should keep my mouth shut, and as a proposal for me to retire." Accordingly, he wrote, "I am compelled to *tender my resignation from the Central Committee,* which I hereby do, reserving my freedom to agitate *in the lower ranks* of the party and at the party congress."[14] The threat sobered his colleagues. Having previously urged—in fact ordered—him to remain in Finland, presumably to protect his safety, they relented and invited him to return. No more was heard of the resignation, and after suitable preparations he arrived in the capital on October 20, again disguised as a locomotive fireman. After a reunion with Zinoviev, who had been back in Petrograd for some time, he walked to his new domicile, the apartment of Margarita Fofanova, a Bolshevik deputy in the Petrograd Soviet and a friend of Krupskaya.

With hardly a pause Lenin set to work, as he had in April, to recapture the party—or at least the Central Committee. The decisive confrontation took place on October 23 in an overnight session at the apartment of a minor party member, ironically the wife of Nikolai Sukhanov, the garrulous Menshevik chronicler of the Russian Revolution. Only sketchy accounts exist of the heated discussion (Sukhanov, unfortunately for later historians, was absent). But the substance is well known: the implacable Lenin, with a terrible sense of urgency for fear the party might let slip its historic opportunity, emerged once more with a victory. Of twelve committee members present, only two—Zinoviev and Kamenev—opposed him on the final vote. Lenin himself, using the "gnawed end of a pencil on a sheet of paper from a child's note-book ruled in squares," hastily wrote down the majority resolution.[15] Although the principle of armed insurrection had been accepted, no date was specified and no preparations made. Nor did the committee majority or the Bolshevik cadre fully share the confident zeal that motivated their leader. There were rumblings of discontent, a pervasive anxiety that the party had embarked upon a reckless gamble and that Lenin's strategic plan, as one middle echelon activist put it, "limps on all four legs." Lenin was aware of these "vacillations" and rebuked the "melancholy pessimists" who wanted to abandon the struggle before it had begun. In the recollections of these Cassandras, as Trotsky tersely summed it up, "the doubts are painted in with water colors and the confidence in heavy oil."[16]

The projected seizure of power had not advanced appreciably when a party conference met on the evening of October 29 for a further airing of the essential question. With Sverdlov presiding, the twenty-five delegates argued until morning. Zinoviev and Kamenev stood by their earlier opinion and again formed a two-man minority. Lenin was infuriated that his closest collaborators had deserted him, and when they committed the unpardonable offense of publishing their objections in the non-Bolshevik press (Maxim Gorky's newspaper) he denounced them for "strikebreaking" tactics and demanded their expulsion from the party. Although the Central Committee accepted Kamenev's resignation, no further action was taken, much to Lenin's disgust. The two "strikebreakers" temporarily withdrew from party work and were subsequently restored to favor, but their "treachery" on the eve of the Bolshevik Revolution was to haunt them as long as they lived. It was their misfortune that events soon demonstrated the error of their ways with such naked clarity. Yet the steadfast courage with which they defied Lenin—no mean achievement in his frenzied mood—suggests that they were something more than "spineless intellectuals," especially when other party leaders shared in some degree their doubts and hesitation but deferred to Lenin's superior authority and the repetitive force of his arguments.

It was providential for the Bolsheviks that they found in Trotsky a revolutionary organizer of genius, for Lenin's role was necessarily circumscribed by his status as a "wanted but fugitive state criminal," to use Kerensky's melodramatic phrase. Stalin's tribute to his future rival (made nearly a year later in he party press) puts the matter succinctly: "All the practical work of organizing the insurrection was conducted under the direct leadership of the president of the Petrograd Soviet, Comrade Trotsky." The traditional view, which may not be entirely correct, is that Trotsky's vital contribution was made through the Military Revolutionary Committee, a Soviet body originally established by the Mensheviks and taken over by the Bolsheviks late in October as their tactical command center. The full committee, of which Trotsky was (or claimed to be) chairman ex officio, met only two or three times, but the fiction was carefully preserved that it remained a Soviet organ when in reality it was virtually indistinguishable from the Bolshevik Military Organization. Trotsky, among others, preferred to take power in conjunction with the Second Congress of Soviets, scheduled to meet on November 7. He anticipated that it could be done "legally"—and perhaps peacefully—but that the Provisional Government would be unlikely to surrender its authority without a show of force. Lenin strenuously opposed further delay but by the end of October had seemingly resigned himself to Trotsky's timetable.

Soviet historians convey an aura of inevitability about the Bolshevik Revolution—of staunch and confident leadership, of precision planning and clockwork execution, of nearly unanimous enthusiasm by the workers and soldiers of Petrograd. Such is the stuff of legend. Party members, both high and low, were uneasy and troubled, fearful of "reaction" and prone to overestimate the government's strength. Neither side could depend upon a sizable body of troops, certainly none with the fighting skills and esprit de corps of crack professionals. The local regiments were no more eager to engage in civil war than they were to fight Germans, and their passive neutrality was a signal asset to the Bolshevik cause. The reactivated Red Guard, sailors from Kronstadt, and a few units of the garrison constituted the party's striking force. It was a puny and unreliable revolutionary army, but to nearly everyone's surprise it proved more than adequate, not only to seize the capital but to do so with ridiculous ease and minimal bloodshed.

It was all so simple (according to the instant wisdom that hindsight confers so gratuitously) that the kaleidoscope of revolutionary Petrograd is hard to retrieve with accuracy and objectivity. Even the "accepted" version, made sacrosanct by repetition, of a coordinated and prearranged coup d'état on November 7 is subject to question—or at least qualification. No records are available to indicate that the Central Committee or any other party organ formulated a battle plan or agreed to a definite time and date to launch a bid for power. Signs of equivocation and improvisation are more evident than those of resolute determination.

Lenin, fretting in his apartment hideout and unable to obtain reliable information, dashed off a frantic appeal to the Central Committee on the evening of November 6: "The situation is critical in the extreme. Indeed it is clearer than clear that now a delay in the uprising would be equivalent to death. . . . It would be an infinite crime on the part of revolutionaries if they let this moment slip by. . . . The government is tottering. It must be *finished off* at any cost!"[17] He was unaware that government and Bolshevik forces were already engaged in a probing action for the control of the key public buildings and installations. In every case the meager detachments available to Kerensky, chiefly officers and military cadets, gave way without resistance to the armed workers and soldiers mustered by the Bolsheviks. Only when these surprising reports reached Smolny Institute, a former school for girls that now served as party headquarters, did the Military Revolutionary Committee contemplate a full-scale offensive.

Lenin's arrival at Smolny a few hours after sending his plea for a showdown may have been decisive, for no one, not even Trotsky, appeared ready to enlarge these tentative skirmishes into a definite test of strength. Dressed in a shabby overcoat and cap, Lenin had left the Fofanova apartment accompanied by Eino Rakhia, who had been serving as a bodyguard and messenger. They boarded a streetcar for part of the trip, crossed a bridge spanning the Neva River on foot, and began the long walk to Smolny at the eastern edge of the city. Two mounted cadets stopped them briefly, but they bluffed their way past and arrived at their destination about midnight. Unfortunately, the memoir literature, so abundant on trivial aspects of Lenin's career, tends to languish at this critical juncture. But presumably he picked up the reins of party command with zest: at last, after frustrating weeks of semi-isolation and blistering exhortations that were ignored or "interpreted" in strange ways, he could confront his recalcitrant colleagues in person.

The air of uncertainty disappeared, and by morning the Winter Palace, the seat of the Provisional Government, was the only major enclave in Bolshevik Petrograd. Trotsky recalls a sleepless night and messengers arriving every five or ten minutes with some new scrap of information. A tired but smiling Lenin remarked, "You know, from persecution to a life underground, to come so suddenly into power. . . ." He searched for the right phrase and concluded in German while his hand circled his head in an expressive gesture: "*Es schwindelt*—one gets dizzy."[18]

In a proclamation to the "citizens of Russia" dated November 7, 10 A.M., Lenin declared that state power had passed into the hands of the Military Revolutionary Committee. His announcement was a trifle premature, for the Winter Palace still held out. Infuriated at the delay, Lenin paced around his room at Smolny "like a caged lion" and threatened to have his military aides shot.[19] The Second Congress of Soviets, scheduled to meet at noon, was postponed until evening. Finally, well after midnight, the palace was taken by tactics of infiltration and intimidation rather than those of frontal assault.

To seize Petrograd was not to seize Russia, and Lenin had a lively awareness that Bolshevik rule, like that of the Paris Commune in 1871, might be short-lived. But the opposition was fragmented and uncertain. Only in the spring of 1918 did it rise in armed rebellion, and a savage civil war followed that belied the almost effortless victory won just a few months before.

CHAPTER VII

Building the Socialist State

RUSSIA BECAME, BY RIGHT OF REVOLUTION, THE WORLD'S FIRST SO-
cialist state. But even Lenin, whose doctrine was pliable enough
to accommodate the staggering problems that arose in building
"socialism" in a backward land, never professed to believe that
Russia could become a Marxist redoubt in a capitalist Europe.
Although something of a nationalist (at least more so than a
"Westernized" Bolshevik like Trotsky), he never doubted that
the Russian Revolution was but a prelude to a great rising of
the European proletariat. That the "toiling masses" of the West
would be unworthy of the confidence placed in them never seriously occurred to the Bolshevik leaders, so bemused were they
by their own sudden victory as a certain harbinger of militant
socialism on a global scale.

Before dawn on November 8, while most of the exhausted party
leaders at Smolny fell asleep "like hibernating bears," Lenin left
for the nearby apartment of Bonch-Bruyevich. Worn out and still
feeling the nervous strain of the past thirty hours, he slept fitfully
and soon arose to work at a desk in his bedroom, drafting the
decrees that he intended submitting to the Soviet congress. Later
that day the Central Committee met to form the new government. Since the word "minister" retained a bourgeois flavor
the cabinet members became "people's commissars" (Trotsky's
suggestion), and the executive body, designated the Council of
People's Commissars, also secured Lenin's approval: "That's
splendid; smells terribly of revolution!"[1] As was to be expected,
Lenin became chairman of the Council (in effect, prime minister), while Trotsky was chosen commissar for foreign affairs.
The other appointees were hardly known outside the party, and
the omission of Zinoviev and Kamenev may have been a concealed reprimand for their recreant behavior before the seizure of

power. But nothing came of Kamenev's "resignation," nor did Lenin revive his demand that they be ousted from the party.

Preoccupied with the capture of the Winter Palace, Lenin had missed the first session of the Congress of Soviets. The deputies convened again on the evening of November 8 without the Mensheviks and Socialist Revolutionaries, most of whom had quit the session in protest the previous day. Lenin's appearance was greeted by thunderous applause. The pro-Bolshevik American journalist John Reed has furnished the classic eyewitness description: a "short, stocky figure, with a big head set down in his shoulders, bald and bulging. Little eyes, a snubbish nose, wide generous mouth, and heavy chin; clean-shaven now, but already beginning to bristle with the well known beard of his past and future. Dressed in shabby clothes, his trousers much too long for him." Rising to speak later on, he gripped the "edge of the reading stand, letting his little winking eyes travel over the crowd as he stood there waiting, apparently oblivious to the long-rolling ovation, which lasted several minutes." He then said simply, "We shall now proceed to construct the Socialist order!"[2] (An appropriate opening remark, the official minutes fail to record it, and Reed may have been exceeding his poetic license.)

Lenin read a decree on peace calling for an armistice and immediate negotiations by all belligerents and, as a gesture to the revolutionary nature of the new regime, with a special appeal to the workers of Great Britain, France, and Germany for "vigorous action" that would help bring an end to hostilities. It also promised that the secret treaties signed by the tsarist regime with the Allied powers and never repudiated by the Provisional Government would be published in full. A moderately phrased document compared to Lenin's more strident pronouncements, it refrained from the more obvious kinds of revolutionary preachment and did not even suggest that socialism was the proper cure for a capitalist war. It was intended primarily for domestic consumption—Lenin knew that a favorable response by the warring powers was a remote possibility—and its message was directed mainly to the politically uncommitted who longed for peace and whom the Kerensky government had alienated with such little regard for its own future.

Lenin also read a decree on land that redeemed the party's pledge to the peasants while unashamedly appropriating the

Socialist Revolutionary program. Private ownership of the land was abolished and placed at the disposal of local committees and peasant Soviets, which meant in practice that the land seizures of the past six months were legalized. In short, the *muzhik's* immemorial land hunger was satisfied in the short run, but his future was mortgaged (though he scarcely realized it) to the needs of "socialism" as defined by the party. He was not to discover that he had been "cheated" until Stalin's drive to collectivize the farms in 1929. There is unintended irony, therefore, in Lenin's statement (apparently made in all sincerity) that the "creative faculties of the masses" should be allowed "complete freedom." The peasants would solve the agrarian problem: "[They] should be firmly assured that there are no more landowners in the countryside, that they themselves must decide all questions, and that they themselves must arrange their own lives."[3]

Both decrees were ratified with virtual unanimity, and a Central Executive Committee of 101 (later greatly enlarged) was chosen to serve as an interim legislature until the next Soviet congress. The Left Socialist Revolutionaries, who had formally split with their party center, received generous representation, and three of their number took seats in the Council of People's Commissars in December. The appearance of a coalition government was thus preserved, but Lenin was determined to maintain Bolshevik authority and had faced bitter opposition in the Central Committee on precisely that point. Five members resigned in protest on November 17, unwilling to countenance a party dictatorship. Lenin denounced them as "deserters" and recalled the previous strikebreaking activities of Zinoviev and Kamenev (two of the dissenting five). Zinoviev soon recanted—the others after a longer interval—and all were eventually reinstated. Lenin, though quick to anger on matters of party discipline, was surprisingly tolerant of transgression when the penitent sought absolution.

The Central Committee of twenty-one remained the key party organ, its duties vastly augmented, for party business was now largely government business. The legal façade of a Congress of Soviets and a Council of People's Commissars obscured but did not conceal the ultimate source of political power. Lenin, as "first among equals" in the Central Committee, was in a de facto sense Russia's new ruler—and even its "dictator." Yet the term implies such unbridled power (on the order of Stalin's two decades later) that it would be misleading to assume that he possessed unquestioned supremacy, even among his faithful supporters. Free debate and democratic voting procedures still prevailed at all levels of the party structure, and he continued to abide by these rules even when, as occasionally happened, he found himself in the minority.

Few Bolsheviks had any administrative experience outside the party. To many, the sudden transition from professional revolutionary to government bureaucrat was a traumatic experience. And to compound the normal difficulties besetting any new regime, the state employees were almost uniformly hostile to their Bolshevik masters and conducted a somewhat disorganized general strike that dragged on for many weeks. But despite these handicaps the party hierarchy had a sense of high purpose and lofty resolve, conscious of the historic role it was playing and determined to apply Marxist doctrine to Russian conditions while awaiting the "inevitable" European revolution. A flood of decrees, some unbelievably petty and others of historic importance, poured forth from the neophyte Soviet government—in sharp contrast to the vacillation and delay that characterized its predecessor. A great many were more than legal and administrative edicts: the propaganda content was deliberately inflated to impress the population with the goals and accomplishments of Bolshevik rule.

As always, Lenin was a hard taskmaster but expected no more of others than he did of himself. He held lengthy cabinet meetings almost daily, presiding with firm authority. He limited debates, allowing no more than ten minutes to an opening report on a given topic, and frequently scribbled notes of inquiry to his colleagues. He would sum up the discussion with a tone of finality, and ordinarily these remarks would form the basis of a fresh decree. His office as well as his living quarters were located at Smolny—on different floors and connected by a private elevator. Occasionally, when time permitted, he would stroll outside the building with Krupskaya, who held a full-time job, first in local government and later in the Commissariat of Education. Security measures were somewhat haphazard, but a patrol of Red Guards discreetly kept them in sight. Later, in mid-January, an unknown assassin fired at Lenin's car and slightly wounded his fellow passenger, the Swiss socialist Fritz Platten.

A spirit of egalitarianism prevailed among the new Russian oligarchs. As austere Marxists they disdained bourgeois amenities, at least those pertaining to creature comforts. But inflation, transport difficulties, and food shortages disrupted the economy under nascent socialism, as it had under capitalism, and tea, soup, and black bread were the staples of life to rulers and ruled alike. If conditions failed to improve—they became, in fact, a good deal worse—the impoverished masses were able to derive psychological satisfaction from the abrupt loss of status and affluence by the propertied and educated. Yet for all their deliberate pandering to the baser instincts of the illiterate and semi-literate, the Bolsheviks did not extend their revolutionary idealism to such extravagant notions as wage equality or the assignment of ordinary workers to run the state—or even the factories.

One anecdote has survived conveying Lenin's skepticism on the subject of instant socialism as a panacea for economic ills. A delegation of workers came to ask that their factory be nationalized. Lenin explained the procedure, but before signing the necessary form he asked if they knew where to get the proper raw materials. They reluctantly admitted their ignorance. "Do you understand the keeping of accounts and have you worked out a method for keeping up production?" he allegedly inquired. No, they confessed that they were not well informed about such things either. "May I ask you," he went on, "whether you have found a market in which to sell your products?" Again the answer was in the negative. "Well comrades," he said, "don't you think you are not ready to take over your factory now? Go back home and work over these matters. You will find it hard; you will make many blunders, but you will learn. Then come back in a few months and we can take up the nationalizing of your factory."[4] Lenin ridiculed those "blockheads" who maintained that engineers, managers, and other technical experts were simply highly paid capitalist drones. While it could be plausibly argued that he had only recently been under that misapprehension himself, he rapidly shed his utopian illusions and with extraordinary flexibility became a hard-nosed pragmatist. At times he sounded more like a thrifty capitalist than a radical socialist: "Keep accurate and honest accounts of money," he advised the Russian people in the spring of 1918. "Manage economically, don't loaf, don't steal, keep the strictest labor discipline." Such instructions, "justly scorned by the revolutionary proletariat when the bourgeoisie used them to conceal its rule as an exploiting class," should become the "principal slogans" during the transition to a socialist order.[5]

The ambivalence of the Central Committee on measures of repression against the opposition was illustrated most dramatically by the case of the Constituent Assembly. This illusory legislature at last approached corporeal status when a nationwide election was held on November 25 (in some districts at a later date). The Bolsheviks, having loudly and repeatedly abused the Provisional Government for its procrastination, refrained from interfering. No friend of "bourgeois democracy," Lenin had recommended postponement to manipulate the voting procedure (Kadets and "Kornilovites" could at least be disfranchised). But he received no support, and the election returns strongly favored the Socialist Revolutionaries. The party of the peasants received about thirty-eight percent of the votes to less than twenty-four for the Bolsheviks, a resounding electoral defeat for the "proletarian dictatorship" clearly foreshadowed by population statistics and the pattern of party loyalty in the countryside. Lenin pointed out, with some justification, that the Socialist Revolutionary split occurred after the list of candidates had been drawn up and that the left-wing secessionists were more truly representative of the peasants than the parent organization. Yet without coercion and fraud on a huge scale, a tactic that was not seriously considered, the Bolsheviks (together with the Left SR's) could not have commanded a majority at the ballot box whatever the formal voting arrangements.

On the afternoon of January 18, 1918, the deputies to the Constituent Assembly, chosen, as Western observers are wont to say, in the "freest election in Russian history," met at the Tauride Palace. They were under no illusion that the Bolsheviks would gracefully surrender to their superior moral authority. Forewarned by the hostility of the press and less subtle acts of intimidation, they brought candles and sandwiches, prepared for a lengthy siege. Sverdlov, rudely usurping the platform, opened the session by presenting a "declaration of rights of the toiling and exploited peoples." Lenin sat nearby, "smiling ironically, joking and jotting down notes" but took no part in the proceed-ings. The declaration was not finally disposed of until midnight (237 votes to 138 for rejection), and an hour or so later the Bolshevik delegation withdrew. The Left SR's followed after an appropriate interval. Shortly before 5 A.M., apparently on Lenin's instructions, the boisterous complement of armed soldiers and sailors "guarding" the assembly forced a recess. When the deputies returned at noon for the second session a decree of dissolution by the Soviet Central Executive Committee, reinforced by troops barring the entrance, suspended the Constituent Assembly for good.

The abrupt dispersal of what was to be Russia's last link with "formal" democracy evoked no answering protest from the masses. The Bolsheviks were secretly relieved, for their popular mandate was insecure, and Lenin's contempt for "parliamentary cretinism" was not fully shared by his comrades or by the "fellow traveling" Left SR's. Performing an autopsy upon these "moribund politi-cians . . . exuding the stale and musty odor of antiquity" at a meeting of the Soviet Central Executive Committee, Lenin de-clared that when he came from Smolny, "that fountain of life, to the Tauride Palace, I felt as though I were surrounded by corpses and lifeless mummies. . . . To hand over power to the Constituent Assembly would again be compromising with the malignant bourgeoisie."[6] (Almost two years later, in commenting upon a published analysis of the election returns, he pointed unerringly to the conditions that made the Bolshevik victory possible: " (1) An overwhelming majority among the proletariat; (2) almost half of the army; (3) an overwhelming superiority of forces at the decisive moment at the decisive points, namely: in the capitals [Petrograd and Moscow] and on the war fronts near the center.") [7]

While Lenin was providing a caustic and rather necrophilic epitaph for a mismatched and thoroughly beaten foe, a far more serious threat to Bolshevik rule—the German army—waited for the politicians and diplomats to cease their labors. The peace decree of November 8 had not been allowed to lapse by default. As expected, it was ignored by the belligerents, and the Soviet government finally admitted (though not in so many words) what the logic of Bolshevik propaganda had always demanded: that Russia would have to sign a separate peace if the war with

Germany was to be terminated. On November 21 fraternization with the enemy was ordered on all fronts, and negotiations soon began at the town of Brest-Litovsk in Russian Poland. An armistice on December 15 led to formal peace talks, but Germany's cynical interpretation of the Bolshevik "no annexations and indemnities" formula (borrowed from the Petrograd Soviet) prevented a quick settlement. If Poland and the Baltic territories under German occupation decided "of their own free will" to break away from Russia and join some other state, it could hardly be classified as a forcible annexation, explained General Max Hoffmann, with the subtle aplomb of the cat "bargaining" with the mouse.

The Bolsheviks had only one trump card to play—the German revolution. Every sign and portent of domestic unrest was magnified tenfold, and the desired conclusion, that given a little more time the German proletariat would prove worthy of its heritage, followed with automatic precision. To gain the necessary time required the services of a skilled agitator, and to spin out the negotiations (and to lend his own prestige to the occasion) Trotsky reluctantly acceded to Lenin's request that he act as Russia's official "delayer." He replaced Adolf Yoffe (a friend and disciple) at the head of the Russian delegation and performed his assignment as diplomat-propagandist with his customary éclat, but the audience he sought, the German people, was virtually inaccessible at Brest-Litovsk. Foreseeing an ultimatum if he persisted with his sarcastic harangues, he suggested, in a letter to Lenin, a bold and unprecedented scheme to blunt the force of German might. What if Russia simply declared the war at an end and refused to sign the peace? An attack could not worsen its already defenseless position and might be a useful "pedagogical demonstration" to the European proletariat of the deadly enmity between the Bolshevik regime and the German imperialists. Lenin was dubious and asked for a more thorough discussion in Petrograd.

Trotsky gained the necessary respite when the Germans consented to a recess, and he returned to the capital on January 18, 1918. For the next few days the Bolshevik leadership was convulsed by a fiery debate over strategy. The advocates of a "holy war" encountered Lenin's cool realism. Who was left in the trenches to fight? But his warning against "intoxication with the revolutionary phrase" was ignored by the so-called Left Communists led by Bukharin. As for Trotsky's formula, eventually abbreviated to "No war, no peace," Lenin considered it too risky and predicted that the Germans would not be bluffed: they would send "specially selected regiments of rich Bavarian farmers." The German revolution, he conceded, was "vastly more important" than the Russian. "But when will it come? No one knows. And at the moment, there is nothing so important as our revolution. It must be safeguarded against danger at any price."[8]

Apparently discouraged by an adverse vote at a party conference on January 21—only fifteen of sixty-three were willing to accept the German terms—Lenin became partially reconciled to the lesser evil as represented by the "neither war nor peace" idea. "For the sake of a good peace with Trotsky," he said with a chuckle, "Latvia and Esthonia are worth losing." At the decisive Central Committee meeting on January 24 the vote was nine to seven in favor of Trotsky's motion. For the opposite extremes of immediate peace or of revolutionary war neither Lenin nor Bukharin could muster much support.

Trotsky gambled and lost. On February 10 he brought off his coup de théâtre at the conference table, only to discover that the German high command had a ready answer to unconventional diplomacy: military power with no moral scruples about using it. An offensive that seemed likely to overrun Petrograd was launched eight days later, and the use of "rich Bavarian farmers" was hardly necessary. German infantry advanced unopposed as the Bolsheviks attempted—too late—to obtain the original peace terms. Although deeply suspicious of the Allied powers, Trotsky sought their assistance and obtained a single vote majority in the Central Committee for his motion in favor of accepting whatever aid might be forthcoming. Lenin was absent but scribbled a note: "I request that my vote be added in favor of taking potatoes and arms from the bandits of Anglo-French imperialism."[9]

The Germans halted their offensive within a hundred miles of Petrograd and presented new and more onerous conditions. The panicky Bolsheviks were meanwhile preparing to evacuate the government to Moscow. Lenin, declaring that it was time to end revolutionary phrase-making, threatened to resign from both the government and the Central Committee if the terms were not accepted. With Trotsky and three others abstaining, he achieved a seven to four majority when the crucial vote was taken among the party leaders on February 23.

The Treaty of Brest-Litovsk was signed on March 3. The Russian delegation ostentatiously refused to discuss the terms, the better to dramatize their helpless submission to a dictated peace. The formalities of ratification were disposed of at the Fourth Congress of Soviets in Moscow on March 16. Lenin, with compelling logic, argued that it was a "revolutionary duty" to conclude this "rapacious treaty," for with only the "sick remnant of an army" it would be self-deception to "accept battle and call it a revolutionary war." He dubbed it a "Tilsit peace" in reference to the humiliating treaty that Napoleon had forced Prussia to sign in 1807, and he implied that Russia's "powerful ally," the "international socialist proletariat," would undo the settlement in the not too distant future. In the privacy of his office, he took the official treaty in his hands and said with a laugh, "The binding is good, the print is beautiful, but before six months are up there won't be a trace left of this pretty piece of paper."[10] He was eminently correct in pointing to the transitory nature of the treaty, but Allied armies, not the revolutionary proletariat, were to deliver Russia from the thralldom of Brest-Litovsk.

In almost single-handedly forcing through a separate peace with Germany, Lenin saved both the Russian state and the Bolshevik Revolution. His qualities as a leader, compared, for example, to the emotional instability of a Bukharin or the touchy egocentricity of a Trotsky, never showed to better advantage than in the tough-minded and dispassionate manner with which he carried the party through its first major crisis since the seizure of power. But his wisdom and foresight, so obviously vindicated in November, had yet to be demonstrated in the spring of 1918. The Left SR's, alienated in the struggle over the peace treaty, resigned from the government in March and continued to agitate for a revolutionary war. The Left Communists were reconciled and remained in the party, though maintaining for several months their factional identity and a "leftist" course on domestic issues.

On March 10 Lenin and other party leaders departed for Moscow on a special train. He and Krupskaya lived at the National

Hotel near Red Square until quarters became available in the Kremlin, that brooding fortress whose massive walls had sheltered the Russian sovereigns until Peter the Great moved the capital to the newly built city of St. Petersburg. With Maria Ulyanova, they shared a comfortable but sparsely furnished four-room apartment. A connecting corridor, occupied until the end of 1918 by telegraphers and their equipment, led to Lenin's office, a moderately spacious room crammed with bookshelves containing nearly 2,000 volumes. A reluctant Lenin was persuaded to use a personal stenographer for a time, but his solitary work habits were too ingrained, and he again resorted to dictation only in 1922 when illness made it necessary. He continued his frugal habits, eating whatever the Kremlin dining room provided (usually rather sorry fare) and assigning the food parcels sent by admirers to schools, hospitals, and orphanages. His suit became so threadbare that Sverdlov arranged for a tailor to be "smuggled" into the Kremlin to fit him for a new one. His salary was five hundred rubles a month—ostensibly $250 at the prewar rate of exchange but badly depreciated by inflation. After it was raised to eight hundred rubles on March 1 he wrote a letter of "severe reprimand" to Bonch-Bruyevich, who was in charge of business affairs for the Council of People's Commissars.

Lenin developed no personality cult during his lifetime, though the Leninist mystique had already taken firm root in the party. He discouraged favoritism of any sort and was repelled by flattery or servility. But he did endure ceremonial appearances and necessary state functions in the belief that the masses would better identify with the new government. His unpretentious manner together with lack of vanity is certainly unique among the rulers of modern history. While obviously enjoying the exercise of power, he was seemingly devoid of personal ambition, successfully resisting the moral corruption that appears to erode the judgment and sap the will of even the most dedicated idealist. Soviet memoirists, occasionally willing to concede a trivial flaw, perhaps to demonstrate that the man was human, convey such a bland and saintly image that the independent biographer inevitably becomes suspicious of unrelenting virtue and seeks (usually in vain) to penetrate to the "real" Lenin. That he sometimes lost his temper and could be brusque to the point of rudeness is well established, although the recorded instances occurred in a political rather than personal context. Nor was he the calm and collected master of every situation, for nervous tension (and attendant psychosomatic complaints) recurred with regularity.

Of greater consequence than Lenin's personal integrity—even his enemies have seldom questioned that—was the effectiveness with which he translated his essential humanity into political terms. Given the obstacles he had to face, particularly the civil war that was soon to begin, he achieved remarkable rapport with the Russian people. In a party dictatorship, with himself as party chief, he managed to transcend his dual role as "dictator" and Bolshevik militant. Yet his duty, as he conceived it, led to unpopular decisions—and others that were impolitic or mistaken. While it would be improper to say that his faith in the proletariat became jaundiced with the responsibilities of power, he did lose something of the revolutionary innocence that characterized the years of exile. To build a socialist society required training, discipline, and even regimentation, not simply the expropriation of the exploiters and the substitution of "workers' control." It was far more difficult to eliminate "ignorance and negligence," he admitted at a public meeting in April, "than to overthrow the idiot Romanov or the fool Kerensky."[11]

One instrument of regimentation (to use no more opprobrious a term) that Lenin would have been ashamed to propose before 1917 was a political police force. But how was the new Soviet power to deal with class enemies, especially those with arms and counterrevolutionary intentions? And what of anarchists, bandits, and miscellaneous "hooligans"? An Extraordinary Commission to "combat counterrevolution and sabotage"—Cheka for short—was established on December 20, 1917, the small and inconspicuous progenitor of what was to become a basic institution of the Soviet state. Felix Dzerzhinsky, its Polish chief, was an ascetic revolutionary of intense loyalty and fanatical zeal but regarded by some of his comrades as mentally unstable. His mission, at first rather modest, expanded with a momentum of its own, though the Red Terror did not become notorious until the Communists (as the Bolsheviks called themselves after March, 1918) were fighting a desperate battle for survival. Lenin then "stressed the inevitablity of terror at every suitable opportunity." The enemies of Bolshevism "run the risk of losing everything," he is supposed to have said. "And yet they have hundreds of thousands of men who went through the experience of war, who are well-fed, courageous; they have officers, junkers, the sons of landlords and industrialists, sons of policemen and rich peasants, who are ready for anything. And here are those, excuse the word, 'revolutionaries' who imagine that we shall achieve our revolution in a nice way, with kindness?"[12]

Lenin's belief that a "people's militia" could be substituted for a regular army expired rather quickly after the Bolshevik Revolution. The remnants of the old army disappeared in the wake of the German offensive, and the new Red Army was initially recruited from volunteers whose limited fighting skills were on a par with those of the Red Guard (now largely defunct). But until the summer of 1918 no sizable "White" army or any other hostile force seriously threatened the Soviet regime. Lenin seemed to have won the "breathing space" he so ardently desired and declared in April that the counterrevolution had been "shattered." Trotsky, who had resigned as commissar for foreign affairs, was entrusted with the creation of a professional army, but there seemed no need for haste.

Suddenly, in the aftermath of an obscure incident at Chelyabinsk, a Ural city on the main line of the Trans-Siberian Railroad, civil war erupted over most of the former Russian empire. A Czechoslovak Legion of some 35,000 men, originally recruited to fight against the Central powers on the eastern front, had been promised safe passage to Vladivostok, where Allied vessels were to furnish transportation. The Soviet government, when it learned of the episode—a clash between Czech soldiers and Hungarian war prisoners—ordered the Legion disarmed, yet there was no possible means of enforcing its decree. The Allies sent troops to "rescue" the Czechs, Socialist Revolutionaries attempted to challenge Communist rule, and several White armies sprang up on the perimeter of the Muscovite heartland.

To compound the military and political crisis, the economy had deteriorated still further, and the "bony hand of hunger" (the notorious phrase of a Moscow industrialist in 1917) invaded the towns as well as the cities. Lenin deliberately fanned the class struggle in the countryside: party workers established committees of poor peasants to inform on grain hoarders and profiteers and to ease the task of requisition by the state. But such tactics were self-defeating, for the peasants who qualified as "poor" were outnumbered by the property-minded. The latter, constituting the so-called middle peasants as well as the kulaks, were unnecessarily alienated, though hardly attracted to the pro-landlord White movement. Puzzled by political labels but still grateful to the regime which had given them the land, they tended to opt for the "Bolsheviks" while opposing the "Communists." The committees were disbanded by the close of the year and an attempt made to conciliate the middle peasants. In a speech on agrarian policy in December, 1918, Lenin argued unconvincingly that the committees had served a useful purpose in curbing the kulaks and preparing the way for socialist agriculture. "The majority of the working peasants," he asserted, "are striving toward collective farming."[13] Even if he meant "poor" instead of "working," such a claim was dubious in the extreme. Few, even among the most poverty-stricken, were attracted to the state-supported collectives, and Lenin himself referred to them in 1920 as "almshouses."

Socialism as applied to industry had been more theoretical than actual. Utilities and other public services, the banking system, and foreign trade were brought (or remained) under state ownership in the first few months of Bolshevik rule, but not until the summer of 1918 did the government mount a major assault on capitalism. All large enterprises were nationalized in the name of socialism and in the conviction that the civil war required drastic measures. Later decrees squeezed out all but the smallest of private concerns. War Communism, as the system came to be known, ended in catastrophic failure, and the havoc wrought by counterrevolutionary armies supported by "foreign imperialism" did not entirely conceal the damage done by Marxist dogma applied prematurely and indiscriminately.

July and August were critical months for the Soviet regime. Lenin, Krupskaya hints, was nervous and depressed. He "no longer wrote anything" and suffered from insomnia. His recreation consisted of solitary walks in the Kremlin grounds and an occasional outing with his wife and sister. A chauffered car was always available, and security arrangements had been tightened following the assassination attempt in January. But he sometimes managed to slip away without a bodyguard. Such was the case on August 30. That morning word came of the murder of

Moisei Uritsky, head of the Petrograd Cheka, and Lenin was urged to cancel two speaking engagements scheduled in the evening. Deciding that there was no cause for alarm, he kept his commitments and was on the point of entering his car to return home when a young woman shot at him at close range. One bullet struck his left shoulder, and a second pierced his neck and lodged near the collarbone. He insisted on being taken to the Kremlin instead of a hospital. Conscious but in pain and suffering from shock and loss of blood, he and others in his entourage feared that he had been mortally wounded. But luckily no vital organ had been hit, for competent medical assistance was unaccountably delayed in arriving.

The would-be assassin, captured soon after the shooting, was Dora (Fanya) Kaplan, a Socialist Revolutionary who acted independently in protest at Lenin's "betrayal" of the revolution. Mentally ill, perhaps psychotic, she had been imprisoned for terrorist activity under the tsarist regime. After interrogation by Cheka officials, she was executed by the Kremlin commandant on September 3. The Red Terror, heretofore fairly circumspect, was unleashed to round up "class enemies" and shoot "counterrevolutionary" hostages already in prison. Lenin, who spent several weeks recuperating, is not on record as to these brutal acts of reprisal, but he was not at all squeamish about mass terror as a political weapon and never doubted the compelling necessity of fighting fire with fire. As he wrote Zinoviev earlier in the summer after the assassination of a prominent Bolshevik, the "terrorists will consider us little old ladies" if we do not "encourage the energy and mass character of the terror against the counterrevolutionaries."[14]

It was this doctrine of terror as a political and psychological weapon that set the stage for the execution of the former Tsar and his family in July, 1918. Sent to the remote Siberian hamlet of Tobolsk by the Provisional Government, the Romanovs had been moved to the Ural industrial town of Yekaterinburg (now Sverdlovsk) after the Bolshevik takeover. There was talk of a public trial for Nicholas, whose crimes against the Russian people would presumably be thoroughly aired, and Trotsky offered his services as prosecutor. But the Soviet leaders had more pressing duties than making an example of the deposed sovereign, and the decision was evidently made by Lenin, in consultation with

Sverdlov and others, to do away with the whole family as White forces approached Yekaterinburg. The details were left to the Ural Territorial Soviet. The Bolshevik chiefs preferred to conceal their own role in the affair, allowing it to be assumed that the local authorities had done the deed without first seeking permission from Moscow.

Lenin's doctors allowed him to resume work on September 16. Still weak, he was persuaded after a few days to take more time to recuperate. A country estate at the nearby village of Gorki was placed at his disposal, and on September 24 he and Krupskaya (with an attending physician) moved into the handsome main building, luxurious quarters indeed compared to the cramped apartments and cheap boarding houses they were accustomed to in exile. Meanwhile their Kremlin apartment was repaired and refurbished, a project that Sverdlov dragged out in a calculated effort to prolong the convalescent's stay in the country. In mid-October Lenin returned to Moscow, retaining the Gorki estate as a convenient retreat, especially on Sundays and during the summer months. The problem of adequate security was never completely solved, for he complained about being "pestered by trifles" and "squandering the people's money," and on a few occasions he again evaded his bodyguard.[15] But even with proper protection he met one further misadventure. In January, 1919, while he was driving out of town to see Krupskaya, then recovering from a serious illness, bandits stopped his car and made off with it, forcing the whole party (including the chauffeur, guard, and Maria Ulyanova) to seek help on foot.

On October 22, 1918, Lenin made his first public appearance since the attempted assassination. He spoke before a meeting of Moscow party workers and sympathizers, his major theme the elusive world revolution. Germany, close to military collapse, had deteriorated in a few months from a "mighty empire" to a "rotten hulk." But his implication that the German workers had produced the transformation was farfetched. There were, nevertheless, revolutionary symptoms, and the Soviet government did its best to subvert the Kaiser's regime, using its embassy facilities in Berlin to channel money and propaganda to the Independent Social Democrats. Yoffe, appointed Soviet ambassador after Brest-Litovsk, was deported with his staff on November 6. He lingered near the frontier in the expectation of being recalled momentarily, for a peaceful transition to "socialist" rule followed upon the Kaiser's abdication three days later. He waited in vain: the new government of "regular" Social Democrats was no more sympathetic to Bolshevism than Kerensky's had been. But Lenin, his face beaming with joy, could hardly contain himself when the news first arrived. His jubilation soon flagged ("facts are stubborn things," he was fond of saying, though he failed to apply his aphorism to the German situation). Yet pessimism was equally unwarranted. Central Europe remained a revolutionary tinderbox whose puzzling manifestations periodically elated and depressed the Bolshevik chiefs for a number of years to come.

Unable to influence the German revolution, Lenin reverted to his émigré habits by wielding his literary broadsword against the enemy. The victim was Karl Kautsky, the leading theoretician of German Social Democracy who had recently been appointed undersecretary for foreign affairs. His offense was the publication of an article (later a pamphlet entitled *The Dictatorship of the Proletariat*) that dealt harshly with Bolshevik policy. Lenin, pronouncing it "disgraceful nonsense, childish prattle, and vulgar opportunism," set to work in hot anger and on October 11 published his preliminary findings in *Pravda*. His full polemic, a substantial brochure, appeared some six weeks later: *The Proletarian Revolution and the Renegade Kautsky*. He had lost none of his gift for colorful invective, and the text is laced with slurs on Kautsky's credentials as a Marxist, though Lenin had once looked to him as a true guardian of the faith. But this "lackey of the bourgeoisie," this "blind puppy sniffing at random," is now declared an apostate—"Judas Kautsky."[16]

Kautsky's major complaint about the Bolsheviks was simply that they had abandoned the precepts of formal democracy. This reproof, while perfectly accurate and repeated in endless variation by an assortment of "bourgeois" spokesmen, seemed to infuriate Lenin when it came from a Marxist source. Didn't Kautsky know that despite "gigantic difficulties" while engaged in a "struggle with the exploiters" that a democracy had been created in a backward country "incomparably higher and broader than all previous democracies in the world"?[17] Considered within the narrow confines of Marxian exegesis, both men presented plausible but not wholly convincing arguments. Kautsky's Marx was a democrat in the Western parliamentary tradition, while Lenin's Marx, if not an early-day Bolshevik, espoused party dictatorship in the name of the working class. The dispute, though somewhat obscured by Lenin's vituperative language, focused on a key issue of twentieth-century politics: democratic socialism versus authoritarian Communism. The Bolsheviks, having already expunged the Social Democratic label from the party name, went on to split the international socialist movement in the conviction that opportunists of the Kautsky school represented, in Lenin's inelegant phrase, only a "stinking corpse."

CHAPTER VIII

Militant Communism

BY THE WINTER OF 1918–19 THE CRITICAL MILITARY POSITION OF the Soviet republic had somewhat eased. The Whites, in temporary collaboration with the Czechs, no longer threatened the middle and upper Volga, and Allied troops, isolated in eastern Siberia, northern Russia, and the Black Sea area, were too few to mount an offensive even had the intervening powers agreed to embark on an anti-Communist crusade. The Red Army, approximately 800,000 strong at the close of 1918, had been whipped into shape, largely by the indefatigable ardor of War Commissar Trotsky, but it would have offered only token opposition to seasoned and well-equipped troops.

Unlike Trotsky and other party leaders assigned to various fronts, Lenin remained in Moscow as the supreme coordinator of political and military strategy. As chairman of the Council of Defense he presided over all but two of the 101 sessions that took place from December, 1918, to the end of the emergency in February, 1920. By telephone, telegraph, and mail he peppered military commanders, political commissars, and his own colleagues (Trotsky most of all) with advice, complaints, and queries. The tone of authority and the scrupulous attention to detail were characteristic of his working style, varying little from the anonymity of exile to the notoriety of the Kremlin. His secretary estimates that his war correspondence, excluding unpublished documents, totaled at least five hundred letters and telegrams dispatched to ninety-seven different locations.[1] But her belief that a careful study of this voluminous material would prove him to be the "founder of Soviet military science" need not be taken seriously. He never aspired to the role of military genius—planning campaigns and manipulating troops. Nor did he claim any kind of expertise in such matters, although he had studied Clausewitz, the celebrated Prussian theoretician, with

[125]

close attention and possessed a good deal more than a layman's knowledge of both formal warfare and guerrilla operations. He pored over battle maps with great care and was obviously well informed on strategic and logistic problems, yet he made no apparent effort to obtain professional guidance or advice on a regular basis. An early and forceful advocate of utilizing civilian specialists, he was somewhat cool to Trotsky's idea of employing former tsarist officers but reluctantly accepted it as a military necessity. Nearly 50,000 of these skilled veterans were persuaded to serve the Red Army under the watchful eye of Bolshevik commissars and made a vital contribution to ultimate victory.

Lenin hoped that the German withdrawal from Russian territory late in 1918 would permit Red forces to gain a foothold in the Ukraine—and perhaps elsewhere—before "Anglo-French imperialism" encroached upon the area. His plans failed, however, not because of intervention by the Allied powers but because the Ukrainian nationalists, though feeble, were at the moment stronger than the Bolsheviks. As with the Germans at Brest-Litovsk, he sought to buy time by appeasing the Allies. If the motivating force of capitalism was naked greed, he reasoned that its political retainers might be willing to recall their troops and cease aiding their White servitors with the promise of Russian territory and generous economic concessions. The United States appeared to be the least predatory of the intervening powers, for President Woodrow Wilson, inevitably an "imperialist" by Bolshevik definition, had nonetheless withstood tremendous pressure from London and Paris before committing American troops to Siberia. Nor did he seem bent on carving out a sphere of influence in the Maritime Province, as the Japanese gave every indication of doing.

Lenin's subordinates attempted to sound out the President in the fall of 1918, but these clumsy efforts were ignored. Finally, on December 24 Maxim Litvinov, the future commissar for foreign affairs, contrived the right approach by appealing to Wilson's idealism rather than to his cupidity. After tentative negotiations in Stockholm between Litvinov and an American representative, the Allied governments proposed an armistice and a conference, including all Russian factions, to be held in mid-February, 1919, at the Turkish island of Prinkipo near Constantinople. Moscow's acceptance held out the prospect of numerous economic advantages, including a settlement of the foreign debt that the Bolsheviks had repudiated, and Lenin telegraphed Trotsky that he would "have to go to Wilson." Since "Wilson" (presumably a symbol for the "imperialists") had designs on "Siberia and part of the south," he suggested that Trotsky "exert every effort to take Rostov and Chelyabinsk and Omsk within a month."[2] But the Whites, encouraged by the French, refused to consort with "red-handed murderers and assassins," and the chance for peace was lost.

The Allied governments, preoccupied with peace terms for Germany but troubled by Bolshevik infection in Europe, could easily have arranged a meeting at Prinkipo or anywhere else had they threatened to stop subsidizing the White regimes. This they would not do—the only matter of substance pertaining to Russia that found ready agreement. The French, verbally the most belligerent of the interventionists, were obliged to withdraw their troops and sailors from the Black Sea area in April, 1919, when disaffection and mutiny rendered them useless for combat duty. The Allied venture in northern Russia (at the ports of Archangel and Murmansk) was scarcely better off, though formal evacuation was delayed much longer. The French debacle was overshadowed by the spring offensive of Admiral Alexander Kolchak, the "supreme ruler" of the White forces, who conferred a superficial unity upon the anti-Bolshevik cause. With headquarters in Omsk and equipment furnished by the British, his army advanced westward toward the Volga cities of Kazan and Samara with every prospect of sweeping on to Moscow. Since the collapse of the Soviet regime seemed only a question of time, the Allies made no further peace overtures.

Neither a competent military commander nor an effective politician, Kolchak presided over a ramshackle operation that buckled when the Reds applied pressure to his overextended flank late in April, and it began to disintegrate when they mounted a sustained offensive. Lenin advocated a "hot pursuit," telegraphing the Military Council on the eastern front on May 29: "If we do not conquer the Urals before winter, I consider that the revolution will inevitably perish. Exert every effort. . . . Pay close attention to reinforcements; mobilize the population near the front to a man; keep a watch on political work; telegraph results to me weekly in code."[3] Deceived, as were many others, by the outward strength of Kolchak's forces, he was gratified by the rapid progress of the Red Army, and by July 1 he was able to send "warm greetings to the liberators of the Urals." The campaign in Siberia, though somewhat more difficult than a military promenade, became a rout after the capture of Omsk on November 14.

Trotsky, who spent most of the summer on the Ukrainian front, had opposed the Siberian offensive. Overruled, he suffered further humiliation when "his" commander-in-chief, Yoakim Vatsetis, was replaced by Sergei Kamenev, a former colonel in the tsarist army whose prestige had soared with the Urals victory. Trotsky, his pride hurt, resigned as war commissar early in July, knowing that the party could ill afford to lose his services. The incident could only have reinforced Lenin's distaste for the prickly vanity of his brilliant colleague. The Central Committee formally rejected Trotsky's resignation with a conciliatory statement, and Lenin sought to mollify him further with a signed "blank check" endorsing any military order that he might wish to give.

The White army of Anton Denikin, a former tsarist general, proved sturdier than Kolchak's, though subject to the same disabilities by its failure to win over the civilian population. Toward the end of June, too late to coordinate his drive with that of the spent Siberian Whites, Denikin's forces seized Kharkov, the metropolis of the eastern Ukraine, and Tsaritsyn (later Stalingrad), the key to the lower Volga. Lenin, as usual, badgered his commanders and directed Trotsky to defend Kiev and Odessa to the "last drop of blood," for the "fate of the entire revolution is in question." But those cities too were occupied late in August as Denikin began a push toward Moscow directly from the south.

In mid-October, with the capital in peril, the Northwest Army of Nikolai Yudenich, a White commander also supplied by the British, launched an attack on Petrograd from his Estonian base. Of limited strategic value, "Red Peter" still possessed psychological importance as the cradle of the revolution, and opinion was divided as to whether it could—or should—be saved. Lenin, never the sentimentalist, refused to weaken the southern front and recommended that Petrograd be abandoned to its fate. But Trotsky finally convinced him that even without reinforcements it could be successfully defended and arrived by train in the stricken city on October 16. Zinoviev, the local party boss, was panicky, and Trotsky, with his compelling leadership and driving energy, restored confidence in the garrison and prepared for a siege that, if necessary, was to be fought behind street barricades. Prepared for all contingencies, Lenin ordered the evacuation of government records, the destruction of power stations, and the disabling of the Baltic fleet should retreat be unavoidable. Disregarding his previous judgment, he dispatched reserves from the front south of Moscow and prompted Trotsky: "Yudenich must be finished off *quickly;* then we will turn *everything* against Denikin."

By October 23 Trotsky had not only triumphantly fulfilled his basic assignment but the Reds went over to the offensive, pursuing the demoralized Whites back to Estonian soil. In the interim Denikin's army had been pushed back from Orel, within 240 miles of Moscow, and the retreat degenerated into a rout as disastrous as that of Kolchak. The Soviet republic, if not yet secure, was at least delivered from its most formidable adversaries. In a speech celebrating the second anniversary of the Bolshevik Revolution, Lenin expressed what must have been the heartfelt sentiment of his audience: "After what we have endured no difficulties hold any terrors for us."[4]

With no outward signs of disenchantment, the party leaders continued to make optimistic pronouncements about the state of the world revolution. They had at least taken the initiative of founding a Third International on the ruins of the Second, and if Lenin's statement that Communism had "become the main force in the labor movement of all countries" was pure hyperbole, the year's record was not wholly discouraging. It had begun on an ominous note: the newly founded German Communist Party, the first outside Russia worthy of the name, had received its baptism of fire in the streets of Berlin in January, 1919, an inauspicious debut that came close to political suicide. This ill-advised and badly managed insurrection, which the provisional Social Democratic government suppressed with ease, led to the murder of party leaders Karl Liebknecht and Rosa Luxemburg. Lenin addressed a protest rally, expressing contempt for German "democracy" as "camouflage for bourgeois robbery and the most savage violence." On January 21, in a "letter" to the workers of

Europe and America published in *Pravda*, he denounced the "foul and abominable character of the butchery perpetrated by alleged socialists." Luxemburg, with whom Lenin had ideological differences, was not an uncritical admirer of Bolshevism, and one could have anticipated sharp exchanges between the two had she survived. Her posthumous pamphlet, *The Russian Revolution* (1922), was sternly disapproving of the anti-democratic features of Lenin's rule.

The death of the two German Communists, certainly a tragic blow to the European revolution as Lenin conceived it, was not without some compensatory benefit to the Russians. Aside from their instant martyrdom as victims of Social Democratic treachery, they could raise no objection (Luxemburg had already done so) to the formation of a Communist International. On January 24, 1919, Lenin's long frustrated scheme took formal shape in a document composed by Trotsky—part invitation and part manifesto—that mentioned thirty-nine organizations considered sufficiently militant to participate in the founding congress. It bore the signatures of Lenin and Trotsky for the Russian party, and seven other Communists or fellow travelers then resident in Moscow signed on behalf of various national parties without any mandate to do so.

The "preparatory" session of the Communist International (Comintern) opened in the Kremlin on March 2, 1919. Cut off by the Allied naval blockade and ravaged by civil war, the Soviet republic was not easily accessible. Only three "outsiders" managed to attend of the fifty-two delegates present for the occasion, and only four (aside from the Bolsheviks) were legitimate spokesmen for active parties. Inevitably it became a Russian-dominated affair, and the unanimity of the occasion was hardly marred when Hugo Eberlein, the lone German delegate, abstained from the formal vote that officially established the Comintern on March 4. Lenin apparently handpicked the officers from behind the scenes: Zinoviev became president, and Karl Radek, the party's "German expert," then in a Berlin prison cell, was chosen secretary as a gesture of defiance toward his Social Democratic captors. His interim replacement, Angelica Balabanov, quarreled with Zinoviev and soon resigned.

Lenin's key role at the first congress was disguised, partly by limiting his platform appearances. He opened the first session with a brief but euphoric estimate of revolutionary prospects: "Although the bourgeoisie still rages and they may yet kill thousands of workers—victory will be ours, the victory of the worldwide Communist revolution is assured."[5] On March 4 he presented his "Theses and Report on Bourgeois Democracy and the Dictatorship of the Proletariat," a rhetorical document that explored in some detail the familiar refrain that "freedom" was but a cover for a "foul and venal system" allowing the "rich to get richer" and the "workers to starve." It was accepted without modification but supplemented by a three-point resolution expounding the immediate tasks of world Communism in sloganeering terms. Lenin's concluding speech at the Bolshoi Theater on March 6—also very brief—was couched in the same confident mold. "The founding of an international Soviet republic is on the way," he assured his audience to "stormy applause."

The Comintern's inaugural congress was so obviously contrived that even extravagant oratory and unbridled optimism could not conceal the isolation of the Communist republic and the embryonic status of the world movement for which it professed to speak. Lenin placed the highest priority on the Comintern's activities, dispensing funds with a lavish hand while he and his countrymen endured a spartan regimen. "Do not consider the cost," he wrote the parsimonious Balabanov. "Spend millions, tens of millions, if necessary. There is plenty of money at our disposal." She saw no need for improvident haste: "Expensive agencies with numerous personnel were established overnight. The International became a bureaucratic apparatus before a real Communist movement was born."[6]

The glow of revolutionary romanticism had not dimmed when on March 21 a Soviet republic was proclaimed in Hungary, followed shortly by similar news from Bavaria. Bela Kun, who had been converted to Communism while a prisoner of war in Russia, emerged as the Hungarian dictator in an unexpected and peaceful assumption of power. As the first chink in the Allied *cordon sanitaire* against Bolshevism, Lenin hailed the revolution as one of "world historical importance" once he had established it as authentically Communist. "I haven't a majority in the government," Kun admitted in a radio conversation with Lenin, "but I shall win because the masses are behind me, and we are convening a congress of Soviets."[7]

While the Red Army and partisan units in the Ukraine sought
to relieve the sorely pressed Hungarians, the Bavarian episode
flashed by so rapidly that Moscow could derive only momentary
satisfaction from a jumble of imperfectly understood events.
Founded on April 7 by radical intellectuals and "coffee house
anarchists" in Munich, the Bavarian Soviet republic was initially
dismissed as utopian adventurism by the local Communists. Their
estimate was wholly correct, but the government's swift disintegration, a sense of solidarity with the workers, and the party's
revolutionary honor seemed to require participation in a doomed
enterprise. Lenin, in a message offering "sincere greetings and
wishes of success" on April 27, revealed that he knew almost
nothing about this new "Communist" republic except that it
existed. What measures had been taken to "fight the bourgeois
executioners," he inquired. Had the workers been armed? Had
the capitalists in Munich been expropriated? Had the wages of
farm laborers and unskilled workers been doubled or trebled?
The banks taken over? Hostages taken from the ranks of the
bourgeoisie?[8] Lenin's catechismal exercise, leavened by a perfunctory greeting, could hardly have been received before counterrevolutionary troops stormed the city to exact a bloody toll
from the obstreperous Bavarian "Reds."

Somewhat better informed about conditions in Hungary, Lenin
telegraphed Kun on May 13 expressing confidence that the
Hungarian proletariat, "in spite of the vast difficulties," would
"retain power and consolidate it." Help was still on the way:
"Yesterday [pro-Bolshevik] Ukrainian troops defeated the Romanians and crossed the Dniester."[9] But these partisan bands
were unreliable, and the Red Army was so heavily engaged elsewhere that Kun had to look to his own resources. Pressured by
an Allied economic blockade and attacked by the Czechs and
Romanians, Red Hungary sought to negotiate. Lenin approved
but warned against Western perfidy: "They are deceiving you,
only playing for time in order to crush both you and us."[10] On
August 1, as internal troubles mounted, negotiations proved
futile, and Romanian forces advanced on Budapest, Kun resigned
and fled to Vienna with most of his associates. His blatant attempts to export his revolution to Austria had failed, but the
authorities gave him asylum nonetheless, and he made his way
to Moscow approximately a year after the collapse of his regime.

He became a Comintern functionary and for a time something of a minor celebrity. Lenin, who probably knew better, grossly simplified the causes of the disaster to make a political point. He blamed the "treachery" of Kun's socialist allies: "They vacillated, played the coward, made up to the bourgeoisie, and in part directly sabotaged the proletarian revolution and betrayed it." Of course, he conceded, the "internationally powerful brigands of imperialism" contributed by making good use of "these vacillations *within* the Hungarian Soviet government" and employing "the hands of Romanian butchers to strangle it."[11]

The future of the Comintern and its revolutionary mission looked bleak indeed in the late summer and fall of 1919. At a time of domestic military crisis when the slightest omen from abroad was capable of exploitation by eager propagandists, the European masses remained politically inert. But Lenin retained an unshakable faith in the revolutionary potential of the world proletariat. His frequent complaints about the dearth of foreign news did nothing to alleviate the information vacuum. Newspapers and periodicals were scarce and hopelessly outdated when they arrived, and radio reception was sporadic and unreliable. A network of couriers maintained contact with the West and occasionally brought back first-hand reports despite the difficulty of crossing frontiers. Communist and pro-Soviet organizations outside Russia were similarly handicapped, although the Comintern organ, *The Communist International,* appeared in four languages and was designed to provide news as well as agitprop material. Of the seven issues published in 1919 Zinoviev contributed eleven articles and Lenin seven. Yet the wide distribution that its sponsors sought was never attained, at least in the earlier years of publication, and most European Communists remained unaware that such a journal existed until 1920 or later.

The German party, functioning semi-clandestinely throughout most of 1919, continued to be the linchpin of the Comintern's revolutionary hopes. Its unofficial head, Leo Jogiches, was killed on March 10 under circumstances recalling the brutal murder of Leibknecht and Luxemburg. The mantle of leadership then fell upon Paul Levi, a promising theoretician of limited political talent. He swung the party toward the Right, seeking to avoid the kind of putschist tactics that had thus far brought nothing but disaster. Radek, whose prison regimen was suddenly alleviated in August—he was allowed to conduct a kind of "political salon" from a more comfortable cell—eventually had an opportunity to consult the party leaders. Lacking guidance from Moscow, he independently opposed Levi's plan to force a party split —in effect, to expel the extremists on the Left in a secret party congress at Heidelberg in October. But Radek's plea was ignored, and the dissidents—a large minority—organized a Communist Labor party the following spring. Lenin, though poorly informed on the issues, deplored the schism in a letter to the German majority. His advice had no visible effect: the day had not yet come when a gesture from the Kremlin carried the authority of an inviolable edict.

Lenin's pressing duties as political leader, de facto military commander, chief Marxist theoretician, and the unofficial head of the Comintern did not exhaust his capacity for work. Constantly alert to bureaucratic misdeeds and slovenly performance, he frequently chastised subordinates with "severe reprimands" or warnings of more drastic punishment. "Shooting" became a kind of routine admonition, so diluted by repetition—and of course never implemented—that it merely conveyed his intense annoyance at some particular act of stupidity or gross negligence. Generally tactful in dealing with his closest comrades, he could be caustic and brutally frank with less exalted party members. Lunacharsky, the commissar for education, was censured for the "criminal and negligent attitude" of his department in the handling of statues and monuments. Not even a bust of Marx was on public display, Lenin complained. "Shame on the saboteurs and loafers." Reproof likewise fell upon Vaslav Vorovsky, who headed the state publishing house, for a pamphlet on the Comintern that Lenin condemned as a "sloppy mess," a compilation that disgraced a "great historic event." The guilty parties were to be sent to prison and obliged to paste in the omitted material in every copy.[12] That his one-man crusade against inefficiency and incompetence produced more than an occasional success is doubtful, but his exasperation and threats of prosecution speak eloquently—of Russian backwardness and slothfulness, of stunted civic consciousness, and of Lenin's recourse to bombast and compulsion when the normal channels of persuasion and legal change proved ineffective. But he declined to mount an organized campaign against "bureaucracy," apparently unaware of the staggering dimensions of the problem.

By the winter of 1919–20 Soviet Russia had achieved something of a standoff with the Western powers. Intervention, both overt and disguised, had failed, and Communism, whether of the indigenous or the exportable variety, was not flourishing. In March, 1919, at the Eighth Party Congress, Lenin had not foreseen such a situation. "It is inconceivable for the Soviet republic to exist along with the imperialist states for any length of time," he declared dogmatically. "One or the other must triumph in the end. And before that occurs a series of frightful clashes between the Soviet republic and the bourgeois states is inevitable."[13] But events erode the most confident predictions, and if he found it unnecessary (and impolitic) to repudiate his words, he proceeded on the assumption that the "frightful clashes" could be indefinitely postponed. While never admitting for a moment that the European revolution had receded (though he may have had private doubts), he implicitly accepted the undeniable fact that the Bolsheviks presided over a state and a territory with a historical continuity and a national interest that could be ignored only with the gravest peril to the future existence of the Soviet government. That had been the lesson of Brest-Litovsk, and he was not likely to forget it in less straitened circumstances.

In February, 1920, Lenin granted two "interviews" to the Western press—that is, written replies to a series of formal questions. He stressed the desirability of "peaceful coexistence with all peoples" and, since the Allied blockade had been lifted a month before, a resumption of commercial relations. Shortly thereafter he expressed his satisfaction that "nine-tenths of all external danger to the Soviet republic" had been removed, and by the end of March he was confident that the "pack of capitalist beasts" were "completely powerless to do us any harm" because they had "fallen out among themselves." Nevertheless he sounded a note of caution: Poland, whom the Allies had resurrected as an independent state, had designs on the Ukraine and had been engaged for some time in a war of nerves with Moscow. But he was comforted by the conviction that the revolutionary movement in Poland was "growing" and that its bourgeoisie and landowners were beginning to wonder whether it was too late to attack, "whether there will not be a Soviet republic in Poland before the government acts either for peace or for war."[14] As always, he was bemused if not wholly misled by the indestructible vision he shared with his colleagues of the stalwart European proletariat (with its peasant ally) ready to rise against the capitalist oppressor.

Less than a month after Lenin's speech the Polish army attacked the Ukraine. The détente with the West came to an abrupt halt, and the Comintern (i.e., revolutionary ideology) resumed its accustomed role as the cutting edge of Soviet foreign policy. Ill informed on the vagaries of Western Communism in 1919, Lenin had crystallized his theoretical views by the spring of 1920 and published a pamphlet, *"Left Wing" Communism—An Infantile Disorder,* that inevitably became an inspirational guide and practical handbook for all Communist leaders. Although previously somewhat diffident about applying the Russian experience to the international scene, he now succumbed to the temptation of extrapolating the Bolshevik model as the preferred if not infallible path to revolution elsewhere. But his immediate aim—he seldom if ever wrote a formal essay without focusing on political tactics—was to chastise the "leftists" in the Western parties who refused to participate in parliamentary elections or in trade-union activity. "We must . . . agree to make any sacrifice," he argued, "and even—if necessary—to resort to various stratagems, ruses, and illegal methods, to evasions and prevarication" in order to infiltrate and carry out Communist work in the trade unions. With "bourgeois parliaments and every other type of reactionary institution," he likewise insisted upon boring from within: "Because *it is there* that you will still find workers who are duped by the priests and repressed by the conditions of rural life; otherwise you risk becoming nothing more than windbags."[15]

Lenin's pamphlet may be regarded as a prologue to the Second Comintern Congress. It implied a more rigorous scrutiny of the membership now that the organization had survived a precarious infancy. In June, 1920, Zinoviev frankly announced the necessity of putting "a lock on the doors of the Communist International." Before the delegates gathered for the formal sessions—they began in the latter part of July—the war with Poland took an unexpected turn. Having seized Kiev with comparative ease, the Poles found little sympathy among the "oppressed" Ukrainians and reeled back in the face of a determined counteroffensive by the Red Army. Convinced that the Polish masses would welcome deliverance from their "capitalist-landlord regime," Lenin succumbed to the revolutionary intoxication of the moment and persuaded his associates (Trotsky and Radek were the chief dissenters of note) to authorize a march on Warsaw. He disdained the mere acquisition of territory: the German revolution —and perhaps a Communist Europe—lay like a mirage on the Polish horizon, too tempting to resist.

The Comintern delegates met in a mood of exhilaration, for the advance into Poland was going well. Soviet progress was duly noted each day on a large map in the meeting hall. Numbering over two hundred and representing thirty-seven countries, the delegates were to a large extent genuine spokesmen for existing parties rather than the bogus variety that had assembled for the founding congress. The Russians nonetheless stage-managed the affair with no less authority than in 1919, although the monotonous unanimity of later congresses had not yet become standard operating procedure. Several delegates boldly criticized Lenin's insistence upon rigid organizational discipline and political orthodoxy as overly doctrinaire, and some of the committee meetings were lively indeed. The main business of the Second Congress centered on the notorious "twenty-one conditions" that were to become the litmus test for parties seeking admittance to the Comintern. Lenin drafted the first twenty conditions, and an additional point, proposed by an Italian Communist, was probably the most stringent of all. It required expulsion of all party members "who reject in principle the obligations and theses" of the Comintern. One of the delegates has maintained that a twenty-second condition, "not at all well known," excluded Freemasons.[16]

The conditions were accepted by the congress with only two dissenting votes and prepared the way for a tactical assault on the European socialist parties, most of whom had retained a superficial unity. Behind the scenes Lenin was already at work sorting the opportunist sheep from the Communist goats. Yet his rule of thumb was less ideological than political, and in practice the Comintern proved flexible enough to accommodate a variety of suspect elements provided they were subservient to

Moscow or otherwise useful to his concept of revolutionary strategy. In his attitude toward the German Left, for example, he found it expedient to censure two Independent Socialist leaders, while others, equally "Kautskyan," remained immune because they might be suitable allies in a future party split. Levi, an entirely different case, aroused Lenin's ire because of his skepticism about the German revolution. "After the victorious entry of the Russian troops in Warsaw," Lenin inquired, "how long will it take before the revolution breaks out in Germany?" Levi replied: "Three months, or three weeks; perhaps the revolution won't break out at all."[17] The "at all" put an abrupt end to the conversation and Lenin walked away with a curt nod of his head. That Levi's subsequent disgrace can be traced directly to this episode is doubtful, but Lenin was predisposed to equate prudence and caution with revolutionary faintheartedness. In any event, Levi's grip on the German Communist Party was loosened during the Second Congress.

The delegates held their final session on August 7 as the Red Army prepared for the assault on Warsaw. The Bolsheviks were taken aback when the Polish workers and peasants, far from greeting the invaders as liberators, rallied in defense of their homeland. General Mikhail Tukhachevsky's forces, with overextended supply lines and inadequate reserves, faltered at the gates of the Polish capital and fell back in a disorderly retreat. To anti-Communist Europeans the salvation of Warsaw became the "miracle of the Vistula," a crucial event in the struggle to save Western civilization from the Bolshevik menace. But a Red victory could only have been a fleeting conquest, for it seems improbable that the Western powers would have stood idly by. The Soviet republic was fortunate to emerge from the conflict unscathed, although some Russian territory was lost in the final peace settlement. In gambling for high stakes, Lenin remained indifferent to such grubby details as frontier adjustment. And the Red Army was needed to check the last of the White commanders, Baron Peter Wrangel, Denikin's successor in southern Russia.

For Lenin, the Polish debacle provided a distasteful but salutary lesson: revolution could not be exported with Russian bayonets. He avoided personal recriminations for the numerous military blunders, though he did remark of the First Cavalry's futile sortie in southern Poland: "Well, who would want to get to Warsaw by going through Lvov!"[18] He had only himself to blame for the political decision that underlay the defeat, and he confessed his error in private while maintaining for the time being a discreet silence in public. As for the European revolution, he professed continued optimism, pointing out instances of trade union sympathy for the Soviet position as proof of growing dissatisfaction. "The international bourgeoisie has only to raise a hand against us to have it seized by its own workers," he maintained at a labor congress early in October.[19]

The supposed revolutionary fervor of the Western proletariat had become an indispensable element of the Bolshevik mystique —a kind of self-fulfilling prophecy. If the Hungarian venture had collapsed, the German revolution had never materialized, and the Polish gamble had been a costly mistake, there was always evidence of a sort, however unconvincing to non-Bolsheviks, that the Russian example would be followed at any moment. Lenin could not admit defeat, even in the privacy of his own conscience: to do so would shatter his self-confidence, a vital prop to that indomitable will which sustained an incredible burden of responsibility. There were oblique indications, nevertheless, that within the year following the Second Comintern Congress he lost some of that passionate conviction of imminent revolution and made his peace—though it was somewhat fragile—with the inexorable march of historical events. "Facts have hard heads," he was fond of saying, and he did bring himself to admit that even the "inevitable" revolution might be delayed indefinitely. As in 1907, when he had at last conceded that Russia's revolutionary pulse had grown feeble and devoted his energy to building a "Leninist" party, in 1920–21 he sought to mold the Comintern for the long struggle that lay ahead. Organization, manipulation, and discipline were to be substitutes for mass enthusiasm, and the theory of an international fellowship of revolutionary Marxists ran a poor second to the realities of practical politics, Bolshevik strategy, and Russian leadership.

The Comintern's new "splitting" tactics were rewarded when the German Independent Socialists, meeting at Halle in October, 1920, voted to accept the twenty-one conditions. A substantial majority joined the Communists to provide a mass party of some 350,000 members. In December a congress of the French Socialist

Party sanctioned affiliation with the Comintern, and a majority of the delegates constituted themselves the Communist Party. The Italian Socialists, badly splintered at the Livorno congress of January, 1921, furnished weak opposition to the growing Fascist movement. Roughly a third of the delegates founded a Communist party. The other foreign parties that opted for the Comintern had no claim to a significant working-class constituency. Lenin's hand in these proceedings, remote but effective, had been foreshadowed by the Second Congress. Countering press criticism in Germany and France of Moscow's dictation of the Comintern, he coolly denounced the "outcry" as "sheer nonsense" and a "blatant falsehood" to conceal the struggle between the "revolutionary *proletariat*" and "opportunist *petty bourgeois* elements."[20] His addiction to stereotyped jargon to conceal the nuances of political warfare became, unfortunately, a hallmark of Communist literature that worsened with the years.

In November, 1920, Wrangel's army was smashed in a vain attempt to hold the Crimea. Except for the Japanese, with whom Lenin preferred to play a waiting game, the Soviet republic was delivered from its major enemies. The "siege" atmosphere, psychologically so beneficial to the Bolshevik cause, dissipated just as the regime entered the third winter of its rule. The failure of War Communism could no longer be concealed, and even the party faithful became restless and disillusioned. The peasants no longer feared the return of the landlords and balanced on the edge of rebellion, with partisan warfare against the state requisition squads a frequent occurrence. By midwinter the bread ration, already at a subsistence level for many urban dwellers, suffered a drastic cut, and a fuel crisis caused a temporary factory shutdown in Petrograd. Lenin himself acknowledged the desperate situation. "We are beggars," he confessed in a personal letter on February 19, 1921. "Hungry, ruined beggars."[21]

Dissension in the party, rendered mute by the civil war emergency, flared up with renewed vigor. Many Communists in the trade unions objected to the rigid controls that deprived the workers of any effective management of industry. Dubbed the Workers' Opposition, this faction, led by Alexander Shlyapnikov and Alexandra Kollontai, adhered to a "leftist" position that was more syndicalist than Bolshevik. The opposite extreme—the view that industrial production could be raised only by stern and rigorous measures—found its most forceful advocate in Trotsky. As a "patriarch of bureaucrats" (in Stalin's stinging phrase) he symbolized to the rank and file the growing alienation of the party from its proletarian heritage.

Lenin pursued a moderate course, keeping his counsel on the Workers' Opposition but openly criticizing Trotsky's position. Although ill (apparently from another spell of nervous exhaustion), he spoke on the trade union question at a party meeting on December 30, 1920, and expressed his amazement at Trotsky's "theoretical mistakes and glaring blunders." "Ours is a workers' state *with a bureaucratic twist to it*," he confessed, yet the essence of Trotsky's policy, "bureaucratic harassment of the trade unions," would, he predicted, be condemned and rejected by the next party congress. On January 21, 1921, he frankly admitted in an article in *Pravda* that the Bolshevik leaders were badly split: "We must have the courage to face up to the bitter truth. The party is sick. The party is shaking with fever. . . . Is it capable of healing itself . . . or will the ailment become prolonged and dangerous?"[22]

The disintegration of the economy, the root cause of the party's "sickness," forced Lenin to rethink the premises of War Communism and, indeed, the very essence of Bolshevism as it had been previously understood. Could a revolution accomplished in the name of the working class survive in a predominantly peasant country? If so, could it survive under peacetime conditions when even the "managerial socialism" of the war emergency had constantly flirted with disaster? The Workers' Opposition charged, in effect, that the egalitarian promise of the proletarian revolution had been subverted by the party dictatorship. But Lenin had long since shed his utopian illusions about the efficacy of "worker democracy" as a cure for production ills. By no means ready to abandon the long-range goals of Bolshevism, he conceded that the socialism of classic Marxist theory was not immediately practicable in Russia. At the same time he could not bluntly admit that the revolutionary romanticism of previous party doctrine had been wholly mistaken. He had to quash the "leftists" without mortal damage to the party image. And he had to proclaim a strategic retreat—a partial return to capitalist norms—before the economy collapsed altogether. That Lenin successfully emerged from the ordeal is a tribute to his political genius ranking close to the tactical triumph of the Bolshevik Revolution. But neither he nor the party emerged unscathed: the Leninist "machine" achieved its victories at a cost in revolutionary conscience.

CHAPTER IX

Strategic Retreat and Fatal Illness

ON MARCH 2, 1921, SIX DAYS BEFORE THE OPENING SESSION OF THE Tenth Party Congress, the sailors of the Kronstadt naval base, the "pride and glory" of the Bolshevik Revolution, rose in rebellion. The Kronstadters themselves presented no military threat to the Soviet regime, but the political repercussions were profound, and the psychological impact on the party leadership was traumatic. A spontaneous and elemental protest against the Communist dictatorship and its ruinous economic policy, it was explained away by government propagandists as a White Guard conspiracy (among other improvisations). Lenin, though he refrained from repudiating the official verdict, knew better: "This petty bourgeois counterrevolution is certainly more dangerous than Denikin, Yudenich, and Kolchak put together because we are dealing with a country where the proletariat constitutes a minority and where peasant property has come to ruin, besides which the demobilization of the army has released potentially mutinous elements in incredible numbers."[1]

Lenin feared that the revolt might serve as "a step, a ladder, a bridge" for a White resurgence. More in sorrow than in anger he concluded that forcible repression was imperative if Russia was to be spared the horrors of a new civil war. Trotsky reported on the gravity of the situation at a closed session of the party congress on March 10, and over a quarter of the delegates volunteered for military service. Among them were members of the Workers' Opposition and others whose ideological affinity to the Kronstadters proved no bar to an ostentatious demonstration of party loyalty. Lenin, recalling the fall of Robespierre during the French Revolution, commented: "This is Thermidor. But we shan't let ourselves be guillotined. We shall make a Thermidor ourselves."[2] On March 17, after a ferocious and bloody campaign across the ice of the Gulf of Finland, the fortress was taken. Lenin

[143]

did his best to minimize the affair in an interview intended for foreign consumption. He called it an "insignificant incident," no more likely to break up the Soviet state than were the Irish disorders to threaten the British empire. Some had come to think of the Bolsheviks "as a small group of evil people tyrannizing over a large number of educated people who would form an excellent government upon the abolition of the Soviet regime." "This opinion is completely false," he charged, for there was no one to replace the Bolsheviks except "generals and bureaucrats who have already displayed their bankruptcy."[3]

Lenin's analogy to the French Revolution—a tempting frame of reference for most of the Soviet leaders—was inexact. Yet Russia did experience an economic "Thermidor": the abandonment of War Communism, the restoration of a free market for agricultural produce, and a revival of small-scale capitalism. The decision to conciliate the peasant, to substitute a tax in kind for forced grain requisitions, preceded the Kronstadt revolt by several weeks, although the Central Committee did not give its formal approval until March 7. Lenin submitted his proposal to the party congress eight days later. In doing so he no longer pretended that the collective farm program was going well. "It will take generations," he admitted, "to remold the small farmer, to recast his mentality and habits." The "peasant Brest" (in the words of one delegate) was unanimously approved.

The industrial counterpart of what came to be called the New Economic Policy (NEP) lagged behind the agrarian reform by some two months. Lenin revived the ambiguous term "state capitalism" to refer to the uneasy cohabitation of private enterprise with government ownership. Large-scale industry, banks, utilities, and foreign trade—the "commanding heights"—remained the province of the state, while the peasants and the "Nepmen" operated within the capitalist sector. As a rhetorical capstone to his new creation Lenin launched the slogan "Electrification plus Soviet power equals Communism." Electricity became a kind of status symbol for Russia's planned economy, but the generating plants necessary for more than a token advance toward "Communism" were not forthcoming in Lenin's lifetime.

NEP did little to alleviate the famine of 1921–22 in which some ten million peasants died. The bungling lethargy of the Soviet regime in mobilizing its available food supplies was reminiscent of tsarist inefficiency in the great famine of 1891–92. Lenin had then exhibited a rather callous indifference to mass starvation, blaming the catastrophe on the prevailing social order. He drew no such parallels to this fresh tragedy but admitted in an "Appeal to the International Proletariat" that Russia's "backwardness" had played a part along with "seven years of war, first the imperialist and then the civil war, that was forced upon the workers and peasants by the landowners and capitalists of all countries."[4] Yet it was less the international proletariat than the foreign "capitalists," notably the American Relief Administration, who prevented a doubling of the death toll. The Soviet authorities declared a premature victory over the famine in the summer of 1922 and resumed grain exports. Their precipitate action helped to stabilize the currency and to increase industrial productivity but at an inevitable cost in human lives. Whether tsarist or socialist, the state continued to exact its toll from the rural sector of society. And as long as Russia remained a predominantly agrarian country, the peasants, then as later, bore the brunt of whatever measures of industrialization and "modernization" the government chose to take.

NEP left an emotional scar on the party idealists, particularly those of the younger generation, who found it difficult to accept the kind of political compromises that had become second nature to the leaders under Lenin's tutelage. The troublesome party factions were outlawed at the Tenth Congress, and the "discussion clubs" that tried to carry on the debate were suppressed without ceremony. The Workers' Opposition had been disposed of easily enough, for the Leninists commanded large majorities in the local party organizations that elected the delegates to the congress. Lenin complained of "syndicalist" and "even semi-anarchist" deviations, arguing that the party could no longer afford to become "enthralled in the luxury of studying shades of opinion." The atmosphere of the controversy had become "extremely dangerous," he told the delegates, and constituted a "direct threat to the dictatorship of the proletariat."[5]

The Tenth Congress, while it offered lip service to the concept of democracy in the party and in the trade unions, took a long stride toward the monolithic image that Communism was to project under Lenin's successor. Yet expulsion from the party, the ultimate form of punishment, was seldom invoked in the upper ranks, and the Workers' Opposition, supposedly proscribed, retained a semblance of political cohesion for another year. Inevitably, however, the "organization men" rose to the top of the party pyramid—the *apparatchiki,* whose discipline, loyalty, and bureaucratic expertise tended to prevail over the ideologists and revolutionary romantics. The supreme exemplar of the "new style" Bolshevik was Stalin, the ruthlessly efficient Georgian who became general secretary of the party in April, 1922. Whether the appointment was made at Lenin's request is unknown—Trotsky claims that Zinoviev was the initiator—but it certainly received his approval, for Stalin, unlike his independent and temperamental colleagues, was a man who could be counted on to get things done with skill and dispatch. Trotsky's recollection that Lenin observed forebodingly, "That cook will concoct nothing but peppery dishes," must be regarded with skepticism. The office was then considered one of routine paper shuffling, and no one could have foreseen that its occupant would eventually dominate the party.

The growing ascendancy of the "practicals" was assisted by events outside Russia. Untrammeled optimism about the approaching revolution in the West could no longer be maintained amid the growing evidence of capitalist "reaction." The Comintern, too, was forced into a strategic retreat in 1921. Its attempt to fan revolutionary sparks in Germany had resulted in the disaster of the "March Action," a Communist rising centered in Mansfeld. The German party, gravely compromised, lost a sizable portion of its membership, and Levi, who denounced the enterprise as reckless adventurism, was expelled. Privately Lenin expressed sympathy for him, virtually admitting that he had been made a scapegoat. "If Levi submits to discipline," said Lenin, "bears himself well—he can, for example, write anonymously in the Party press, or write some pamphlets—then in three or four months' time I shall demand his readmission in an open letter."[6] But Levi spurned the role of prodigal son and left the Communist movement.

Those who remained in the German party—a mere 180,000 from the original 350,000—were drawn into a rancorous debate that spilled over into the proceedings of the Third Comintern Congress held in Moscow during the summer of 1921. Lenin blandly declared that the German defeat had been a "great step forward in spite of the mistakes of its leaders." "But this does

not matter," he added, because "hundreds of thousands of workers fought heroically" (only a few thousand had actually been
directly involved) . This inflated rhetoric and other examples of
contrived optimism could not disguise the spiritual malaise of
the delegates compared to the triumphant mood of the previous
congress. "Putschism" and "splitting" were now discarded in
favor of mass participation. Within six months the Comintern
launched the slogan of a "united workers' front" and began to
make overtures to socialist parties whose ideological failings had
placed them beyond the pale only a year before.

Lenin was in good spirits throughout the congress. As informal
as always, he sometimes took notes from the steps leading to the
rostrum and occasionally interjected a caustic comment with a
mischievous smile lighting up his face. The most insignificant
delegates were not beneath his notice, and from time to time he
would genially buttonhole a foreign Communist for a tête-à-tête
in a corner of the hall.

A few grumblings of discontent were heard at the Third Congress about the precedence that the Soviet national interest
seemed to enjoy over the aim of world revolution. It was a theme
that no one dared broach at later meetings when it became obvious that the Comintern had indeed become an instrument of
the Kremlin's foreign policy. In 1921 the issue was still largely
dormant because Russia's normal diplomatic contacts had not
yet resumed. The signing of a trade agreement with Britain on
March 16 of that year was an encouraging sign that the quarantine placed on the Communist state by the great powers was
approaching an end. But the immediate results were disappointing. Not until April, 1922, when the Soviet government was
offered—and accepted—an invitation to the Genoa Conference
on economic problems, did Russia hesitantly emerge from its
enforced isolation. Lenin intended to head the delegation in
person, but poor health prevented his attendance. The conference
itself failed miserably and was remembered chiefly as the occasion
for the Rapallo treaty between Russia and Germany, the beginning of an awkward friendship between the two European
pariahs.

Always solicitous about the health of his comrades, insisting
that those who were especially overworked take time off for an
"overhaul," Lenin shrugged off suggestions that he himself might

benefit from a prolonged rest. Except for an occasional stay in Gorki, he had no real vacation until July, 1921, when illness obliged him to take a month's holiday at his estate. But a heavy workload had become a part of his life style, and he tended to become restless in the relative inactivity of his country retreat. Headaches and insomnia recurred with alarming severity toward the end of the year, forcing him to take formal sick leave. He moved to Gorki and later spent almost six weeks at a state farm near Kostino, not far from Moscow.

Until the Eleventh Party Congress in late March of 1922 Lenin remained in semi-retirement, only sporadically involved in political affairs. His health showed no improvement, and he openly acknowledged to the delegates that it was unlikely that he would be able to return to work in the near future. At least one of his doctors believed that the bullets still lodged in his body from the assassination attempt in 1918 were poisoning his system. Although the theory was highly dubious, the more easily accessible of the two was removed by a German surgeon in a Moscow hospital on April 23. The wound quickly healed, but Lenin's condition became no better. At Gorki on May 26 he suffered a cerebral stroke accompanied by stomach pains and vomiting. His right arm and leg were partially paralyzed and his speech impaired. "For the first time," wrote one of the attending physicians, "death clearly wagged its finger."[7]

Lenin gradually recovered during the summer. Krupskaya provided speech therapy, and the paralysis that had prevented him from writing slowly relaxed its grip. Visitors were permitted in July. Stalin was among them and later reported in *Pravda* that the convalescent had the look of a "veteran fighter who had managed to get some rest after incessant and exhausting battles" but "still bore traces of overwork and fatigue." Forbidden to read newspapers or to talk politics, he nevertheless pressed his visitor for news. Doctors "cannot understand that when professional men of politics get together they cannot help talking politics," wrote Stalin. When he called again a month later the ban on reading had been lifted and Lenin was surrounded by stacks of books and newspapers. There was no longer any trace of fatigue and no sign of that "nervous craving for work. . . . Calmness and self-assurance had fully returned. This was our old Lenin, screwing up his eyes and gazing shrewdly at his interlocutor."[8]

Stalin was guilty of embroidering the truth—of telling the public what it wanted to hear—for Lenin was far from being a well man. But he had sufficiently recovered by October 2 to return to Moscow and resume a work schedule that was limited by his doctors to a five-hour day and a five-day week. However, he seldom adhered to the prescribed regimen even though he cut down his former twelve-to-fifteen-hour day. On October 31 he spoke for twenty minutes to the All-Russian Central Executive Committee, his first public appearance in over seven months. On November 13 he delivered a report in German to the Fourth Comintern Congress on "Five Years of the Russian Revolution and the Prospects of World Revolution," and his appearance was greeted with "stormy, prolonged applause and a general ovation." Radek sat nearby and prompted Lenin with the proper expression whenever his German proved less than adequate. Apparently the speaker was not the "old Lenin" of whom Stalin had spoken so confidently. He was "strongly affected by paralysis," recalls one of the delegates. "His features remained immobile, and his general appearance was that of an automaton; his usual simple, rapid, confident speech was replaced by a hesitant, jerky delivery."[9] But another eyewitness, an American journalist, remembers that Lenin "spoke with machine-gun rapidity in a rather high pitched voice" and mentions no signs of disability.[10]

Lenin's last public address, a brief and rather disorganized "pep talk" to a plenary session of the Moscow Soviet, was delivered on November 20, 1922. A relapse followed five days later, and the doctors ordered a week's rest and forbade work of any kind. Again Lenin made an attempt to comply but was temperamentally unable to give up all political activity. On December 7 he left for Gorki and returned to his Kremlin office on the 12th. It was to be his last working day in Moscow, for he suffered two minor attacks on the 13th and was persuaded to wind up his affairs for another prolonged rest. On December 16, while in his Kremlin apartment, a second major stroke paralyzed his right side, though his speech was not seriously impaired. For all practical purposes his political career had come to an end. Yet he was not resigned to a complete state of inactivity and continued, by reading and dictation, to keep in touch with party affairs and to exert his influence whenever possible.

Lenin's colleagues, however they might revere their fallen leader, must have recognized that his recovery was doubtful. A veiled struggle for power was in fact already under way among the potential heirs—Trotsky, Stalin, Zinoviev, and Kamenev. The colorful Trotsky, assumed by outsiders to be just below Lenin in the Kremlin hierarchy, suffered from a number of disabilities, not the least of them his inordinate distaste for the grubby world of political intrigue. Here Stalin was in his proper element, yet he ran afoul of Lenin during the winter of 1922–23, an unexpected confrontation that threatened to impede if not to halt his growing stranglehold on the party machinery.

To all outward appearances the relationship of the two men had been cordial until the fall of 1922. An annoying but relatively minor disagreement arose over the government's monopoly of foreign trade. Lenin, upholding the sanctity of socialist principle against the inroads of the NEP, won a series of Pyrrhic victories on the question. Settling down to work after recovering from his first stroke, he was chagrined to discover that his wishes had been overridden by the Central Committee and that exceptions to the trade monopoly were now permitted. Unexpectedly finding a supporter in Trotsky, he busied himself with overturning the decision at the next plenary session. Again his view prevailed when the opposition—Stalin prominent among them —backed down. By this time Lenin was again bedridden and dictated a congratulatory message to Trotsky on December 21, 1922: "It seems that we have captured the position without firing a shot, simply by a maneuver. I propose that we do not stop but continue the attack."[11]

Lenin's "offensive" was primarily concerned with what became known as the Georgian question, although he was also troubled by the lagging struggle against the evils of bureaucracy and a dawning awareness of Stalin's grip on the party apparatus. The problem of Georgia pinpointed the disparity between Bolshevik doctrine and Soviet practice toward the non-Russian nationalities. The party had long supported the principle of self-determination for national minorities, including the right of secession, though not without certain ambiguities. But the responsibilities of power—and the exigencies of civil strife—brought awkward compromises and a general retreat from the high ideals of the original Bolshevik platform. While Lenin remained a determined foe of "great Russian chauvinism," it was to Stalin, as the party's expert on nationality affairs, that he delegated most of the day-to-day decisions regarding the ethnic checkerboard of the Soviet borderlands.

During the civil war Georgia had been under Menshevik rule, and the Soviet government recognized its independent status in 1920. But Stalin, who had personal as well as political scores to settle with the Georgian Mensheviks, took it upon himself, abetted by his old crony Ordzhonikidze, to prepare an invasion of his homeland by the Red Army. For a variety of reasons, including the impropriety of military aggression at a time when Russia's relations with the capitalist West showed signs of improvement, Lenin balked at the scheme. By January of 1921 his opposition had weakened under heavy pressure, and he finally gave his consent provided the Georgian Communists staged an uprising convincing enough to furnish a pretext for armed intervention. The necessary arrangements were completed in short order: a revolt of undetermined seriousness broke out on February 11. Three days later the Central Committee formally approved the project, and Lenin sent Ordzhonikidze a cautiously worded message conferring a somewhat hesitant blessing upon the enterprise. The Eleventh Red Army began a drive on Tiflis (now Tbilisi), the Georgian capital, and by February 25, after a brief siege, the city fell. Lenin was sorely troubled by this naked display of force. Perhaps because of a guilty conscience, but in any case to pacify the Georgian people, he insisted upon a lenient and tactful rule accompanied by generous economic concessions. Even the Mensheviks, though anathema elsewhere, were to be conciliated with a view toward a political compromise.

Ordzhonikidze, as Soviet proconsul, gave little heed to Lenin's instructions. He even managed to alienate the Georgian Communists, who, under Budu Mdivani, were prepared to welcome the Soviet "liberators." They objected, above all, to Stalin's proposal to combine Georgia with Armenia and Azerbaizhan in a Transcaucasian federation. Mdivani protested to Lenin that the plan would lead to open rebellion, and it was postponed until a propaganda campaign (mounted in the winter of 1921–22) attempted to persuade the Georgian public of the virtues of the federation.

During the late summer of 1922, while Lenin was convalescing, a constitutional commission was appointed to regularize Moscow's ambiguous relationship with the "independent" border republics. Stalin, who headed the drafting commission, was impatient with the subtleties of constitutional law—those fine points of terminology that served to convince Lenin that the amenities, if not more substantial rewards, had been preserved toward the national minorities. Stalin preferred a unified state, with all political authority radiating from Moscow, though in the end he was perceptive enough to recognize that a federal structure allowing cultural autonomy presented no threat to Soviet rule and might help to reconcile dissenters to a highly centralized and essentially Russian government.

In the fall of 1922, when he was again able to attend to affairs of state, Lenin examined the work of the commission with mounting irritation. The principle of federalism appeared to have been abandoned—and with it the carefully wrought façade of equality and independence for the non-Russian nationalities. Stalin agreed to reconsider but proved surprisingly obstinate about matters of procedure. Lenin found him overly enamored with administrative details and complained also that he had a "slight tendency to hurry." Stalin countered, in a memorandum that bordered on insolence, that "Comrade Lenin himself 'hurried' a little" and that his "hurriedness" would encourage the advocates of national independence.[12]

A revised draft was submitted to the Central Committee, and at its session on October 6, which Lenin was obliged to miss because of a painful toothache, the new version was approved. In a jocular note to Kamenev, Lenin commented: "I declare war to the death on Great Russian chauvinism. I shall eat it with all my healthy teeth as soon as I get rid of this accursed bad tooth."[13]

The Georgian Communists remained unhappy because the proposed Transcaucasian federation had not been dropped. Their complaints went unheeded, and Lenin, who was informed of their refusal to submit to party discipline, on October 21 sent a sharp reprimand suggesting that they couch their protests in a "more seemly and loyal tone." He deferred the argument to the Secretariat—that is, to Stalin—in the conviction that the Georgians were more nationalist than Communist. In despair, the leaders of the Georgian party resigned en masse, and Ordzhonikidze promptly selected a new and compliant Central Committee.

The Georgian opposition, apparently beaten, continued to pester Lenin with a series of messages. Ordzhonikidze was charged with misconduct—even personal violence—and an investigation was requested. Again Lenin turned the complaints over to the Secretariat, and on November 24 Stalin chose a three-man committee headed by Dzerzhinsky to look into the matter. Probably because he doubted its impartiality, Lenin authorized one of his deputies, Alexei Rykov, to conduct a separate inquiry. Rykov's findings have not been disclosed, but Dzerzhinsky reported favorably—as was to be expected—on Ordzhonikidze's Georgian policy. Depressed and visibly upset by the affair, Lenin conferred with Stalin for over two hours on December 13. Illness prevented him from intervening more actively on the side of the Mdivani faction, yet the nationality question continued to agitate him for weeks to come.

After Lenin's attack on December 16 the Central Committee authorized Stalin to see that the doctors' orders were carried out to the letter—in effect, virtually to isolate Lenin from further political activity. Quite likely the element of solicitude in this decision—the party notables were always deferential if not personally fond of their leader—was mixed with some annoyance that an invalid, no matter how eminent, should attempt to formulate policy. And Lenin had been testy, suspicious, and overly officious at times, nor had he been a model patient from the standpoint of his doctors. Even with the utmost tact and good will by all parties concerned, there was no way to avoid an unpleasant situation—a desperately sick man attempting to salvage the remnants of his fading power in the sincere conviction (and perhaps correctly so) that his successors would botch the legacy that was being conferred upon them. Nevertheless, the choice of Stalin for this delicate task was unfortunate, for he had become aware of Lenin's rapprochement with Trotsky and the consequent weakening of his own position.

A prey to uncertainty and fearful that his future was at stake, Stalin committed a tactical blunder by telephoning Krupskaya on December 22 and roundly abusing her for permitting Lenin to engage in political activity (that is, by dictating letters and memoranda). Without informing Lenin of the offensive phone call, Krupskaya sent an indignant note to Kamenev complaining of Stalin's "crude interference" in her private life and his "coarse invectives and threats." "At present I need the maximum in self-control," she wrote. "What can and what cannot be said to

Ilych I know better than any doctor, for I know what upsets him and what does not, and in any case I know it better than Stalin."[14]

The letter, together with Lenin's threat to refuse further treatment, was probably effective in mitigating the strict regimen of the sickroom. At any rate, on December 24 Stalin, Kamenev, and Bukharin conferred with the doctors and agreed that Lenin might dictate his "journal" (as he euphemistically called it) for a few minutes each day provided that visitors were forbidden, that he receive no political news, and that he send no correspondence requiring a reply. As always, he poached unashamedly on his allotted time, and by early January of 1923, as his condition temporarily improved, he was dictating well over an hour each day.

The most significant document of this brief interlude, written when Lenin, though physically disabled, appeared to be in full command of his mental faculties, is usually referred to as his "Testament." Dictated on December 24–25, it forms one of a number of memoranda concerning the future of the party and the Soviet regime.[15] Lenin was especially worried about a potential split in the Central Committee and recommended increasing the membership from twenty-seven to fifty or one hundred, a measure that would, he predicted, increase the stability of the party by a "thousandfold." Presumably differences of opinion would be submerged in a sea of new faces, but the remedy hardly seemed appropriate considering the sluggishness of the existing party bureaucracy. In any event, he considered the immediate danger to be a split between Stalin and Trotsky, "the two most able leaders of the present Central Committee" (a verdict that must have stunned Zinoviev and Kamenev). Stalin, as party secretary, "has concentrated enormous power in his hands, and I am not sure that he will always be capable of using that power with sufficient caution." Trotsky, while of "outstanding ability" and "perhaps the most capable man" in the Central Committee, had "displayed excessive self-assurance and shown excessive preoccupation with the purely administrative side of the work" (seemingly an oblique reference to his vanity and arrogance). As for the other leaders, the "October episode" with Zinoviev and Kamenev—their "strikebreaking" activities on the eve of the Bolshevik insurrection—was recalled as "no accident," but "neither can the blame for it be laid upon them personally, any more than non-Bolshevism can upon Trotsky." If that were truly the case, one wonders why it was mentioned at all. Bukharin, "rightly considered the favorite of the whole party," could be regarded as a Marxist only with great reserve because "he has never made a study of dialectics and . . . never fully understood it." Only one other party member, Gregory Pyatakov, received comment (with the usual plus and minuses), while several of his superiors were ignored. Lenin's frank and unflattering appraisal of his colleagues is interesting for the historical record but puzzling as to his motive. The old principle among autocrats—"divide and rule"—might fit the circumstances except that he was no autocrat (though sometimes autocratic) and unlikely to suppose that he would be able to resume his place at the head of the party. His apparent aim was the negative one of preventing any single individual from assuming his mantle and of perpetuating a kind of oligarchy among the top party leaders.

On December 30–31, 1922, Lenin dictated some notes on the nationalities question in general and the Georgian affair in particular. Could it be that Communist policy was simply borrowed from the tsarist regime and "slightly anointed with Soviet holy oil"? Lenin avoided a direct answer while denouncing Stalin, Ordzhonikidze, and Dzerzhinsky for their part in the unsavory "Great Russian nationalist campaign" in Georgia. Stalin's "hastiness and infatuation with pure administration" had played a "fatal role," and he recommended "exemplary punishment" for Ordzhonikidze despite their personal friendship. As for Dzerzhinsky, though he was less culpable, his report would have to be reexamined because of the "enormous mass of errors and biased judgments that it doubtless contains." It would be "unforgivable opportunism," he argued, that on the eve of the awakening of the Asian peoples, "we were to undermine our prestige there with even the slightest crudity or injustice toward our own minorities." As for practical remedies, Lenin offered a few suggestions, none of which cut to the heart of the problem. Conditioned by his own premises, he was unable to comprehend that "chauvinism" was not simply an alien "bourgeois" excrescence but a built-in element of the party and governmental structure that he himself had erected and maintained over the years. The memorandum, intended for later use, probably at the forthcoming Twelfth Party Congress, was not circulated.

Lenin received additional information of a derogatory nature about Stalin by the beginning of the new year. Most likely it related to the Georgian affair, but possibly Krupskaya let slip some hints about his conduct toward her without disclosing the whole incident. Whatever it was, Lenin deemed it sufficiently serious to append a postscript to his so-called Testament under the date of January 4, 1923:

"Stalin is too rude, and this fault, while entirely acceptable in our midst and in relations among us Communists, becomes unacceptable in the office of general secretary. I therefore propose that the comrades think of a method of removing Stalin from that position and appointing another man in his place who in all respects differs from Comrade Stalin in having only one advantage—namely, that of being more patient, more loyal, more polite and considerate of comrades, less capricious, etc. This circumstance may seem an insignificant trifle. But I think that from the standpoint of preventing a split and from the standpoint of what I wrote above about the relationship between Stalin and Trotsky, it is not a trifle, or it is a trifle that may acquire decisive significance."

The Testament remained highly confidential. Copies were kept in a sealed envelope to be opened only by Krupskaya in the event of Lenin's death. Periodic attacks of headaches and insomnia—familiar symptoms indeed—convinced him at one point that nervous tension lay at the root of his illness and that he might yet recover. In addition to doctors, nurses, a secretarial staff, and a librarian, his sister Maria took charge of household arrangements and various business matters, while the faithful Krupskaya remained in constant attendance. A little stand was placed on his bed, and using his left hand to turn the pages he would check the typescript of his dictated "journal," occasionally making a few corrections.

Lenin put up a gallant fight, not only against the illness that constantly sapped his strength and threatened his mentality but also the difficult task of merely keeping abreast of party affairs. Stalin, not surprisingly, tried to beg off from his disagreeable assignment as the Central Committee's watchdog over Lenin but was ordered (or persuaded) to maintain his vigil. He had learned discretion after the incident with Krupskaya and toward the end of January inquired politely of Lydia Fotieva, the chief secretary, how Lenin kept posted on current business. She denied the role of informant—perhaps a technically accurate statement—and claimed that there was no reason to believe that news was being funneled to him. Stalin asked specifically about the Workers' and Peasants' Inspection (Rabkrin), over which he had presided until May, 1922, well aware that Lenin was displaying undue interest in the past performance of that agency, charged with sniffing out abuses and inefficiency in all branches of government.

Rabkrin, like other Soviet commissariats, had become a swollen bureaucracy, yet not until early 1923, after Lenin had acquired a jaundiced view of Stalin, did he single it out for a public attack. He dictated two articles on the subject: the first, published in *Pravda* on January 23, was mild and unexceptionable, but a second, completed on February 10, constituted a sweeping indictment ("Everybody knows that a more badly organized institution than our Workers' and Peasants' Inspection does not exist"). Although Stalin's name was conspicuously absent, publication would have openly acknowledged that a breach had occurred between Lenin and his hitherto loyal subordinate. At a meeting of the Political Bureau (Politburo), by now the top party organ, the majority opposed publication, and it was even proposed that a fake issue of *Pravda* be printed to satisfy Lenin. This clever but overly crass solution may have provoked a reaction, for Trotsky and Kamenev gained support, and the article ("Better Less, But Better") finally appeared in *Pravda* on March 4.[16]

Lenin, meanwhile, still pursued the Georgian affair with unrelenting tenacity. Dzerzhinsky had been dispatched on a second mission to Georgia and returned on January 27, turning his dossier over to Stalin. After pressure from Lenin, the Politburo consented that it be sent on to him, but the documentation was so voluminous that Fotieva and two other secretaries reviewed the material after receiving precise and detailed instructions from Lenin about what to look for. Their report was delayed until March 3. It was almost certainly critical of the Stalin-Ordzhonikidze policy but has not yet been published.

In casting about for a prospective ally, Lenin turned to Trotsky, who had joined him on the foreign trade controversy and who had agreed to a "bloc against bureaucracy" with Lenin in early

December. On March 5 he dictated a letter to Trotsky that was read to him on the telephone:

Esteemed Comrade Trotsky!
I would very much like to ask you to take upon yourself the defense of the Georgian case in the Central Committee of the party. The matter is now being "prosecuted" by Stalin and Dzerzhinsky, and I cannot rely on their impartiality. Indeed, quite the contrary. If you would agree to undertake its defense, I could be at ease. If for some reason you do not agree, please return the dossier to me. I will consider that a sign of your disagreement.

With the very best comradely greetings,
Lenin[17]

Lenin's memorandum on the nationalities question was sent to Trotsky, and the next day Lenin wrote an encouraging message to the Georgian opposition: "Esteemed Comrades! I follow your case with all my heart. I am outraged by the rudeness of Ordzhonikidze and the connivance of Stalin and Dzerzhinsky. I am preparing for you notes and a speech." He also named Kamenev and Valerian Kuibyshev to a new investigating committee on Georgia.

By this time Lenin had heard the full story of Stalin's offensive telephone call to Krupskaya. Acting somewhat out of character as an outraged husband rather than a disciplined member of the party, he dictated a letter to Stalin on March 5, with copies to Zinoviev and Kamenev:

Respected Comrade Stalin!
You permitted yourself to be so discourteous as to call my wife on the telephone and abuse her. Although she told you that she agreed to forget what was said, Zinoviev and Kamenev heard about it from her. I have no intention of forgetting so easily what has been done against me, and it goes without saying that what has been done against my wife I also consider to have been done against myself. Therefore I ask you to consider whether you are agreeable to retracting your words and apologizing or whether you prefer to break off relations between us.

Respectfully yours,
Lenin[18]

Krupskaya asked Maria Volodicheva, the secretary who had taken down the letter, not to send it. But Volodicheva felt bound by Lenin's instructions and personally handed it to Stalin on March 7. No doubt taken aback by Lenin's peremptory tone, Stalin dictated a letter of apology on the spot, the text of which is still unknown, and Volodicheva returned with it. By this time Lenin was in no condition to read it, for he had suffered another relapse. Three days later a third major stroke disabled him so completely that he never regained the power of speech.

Lenin's incapacity, though it could not be known whether it was permanent, came at a most opportune time for Stalin. Yet it cannot be said with any certainty that the future dictator's career was hanging in the balance. If Lenin had wanted to humiliate him (aside from easing him out as party secretary and blocking him on the Georgian question), he would not have followed the circumlocutious route that he did. He would have denounced him to the Central Committee and demanded his resignation from the party. As in the earlier case of Zinoviev and Kamenev, he simply wished to demote Stalin and to place him on probation. As it turned out, Stalin was spared the embarrassment of confronting Lenin at the forthcoming party congress, where his chances of gaining majority support would have been almost nil.

Insofar as Lenin had named a political successor, it was Trotsky. But presented with a clear Leninist mandate in the matter of Georgia, Trotsky passed up his opportunity and compounded his original error with a singularly inept performance as the troika of Stalin, Zinoviev, and Kamenev combined against him. It would seem that he responded favorably to Lenin's appeal for help on the Georgian question, though the evidence is inconclusive. Fotieva informed him that Lenin was "preparing a bomb for Stalin" at the party congress.[19] But Trotsky had always thought of Stalin as a political nonentity and refused to take him seriously as an aspirant for supreme power. Nor did he relish an open fight. He possessed something of the patrician's haughty disdain about engaging in a political brawl among inferiors. Zinoviev appeared to be his chief rival, and he proceeded to make the "rotten compromise" that Lenin had warned would be the result of any bargain with Stalin. With Kamenev as intermediary, Trotsky indicated that he opposed any drastic measures against Stalin, Ordzhonikidze, and Dzerzhinsky. "I want a radical change in the policy on the national question," he told Kamenev, "a discontinuance of persecutions of the Georgian opponents of Stalin, a discontinuance of the administrative oppression of the party, a firmer policy in matters of industrialization, and an honest cooperation in the higher centres."[20] Stalin accepted the terms with alacrity, no doubt relieved that Trotsky's "Leninism" had sputtered out like a wet firecracker.

On April 17, 1923, the Twelfth Party Congress convened without its leader. But his presence was strongly felt, so much so that the cult of Lenin was founded while the object of veneration was still alive. Press reports managed to convey the impression that Lenin was expected to recover, and Kamenev, who opened the congress, was even more optimistic. That he and his associates really believed these reassurances seems highly unlikely, for they were presumably well briefed by the attending physicians. The delegates, as well as the general public, were obviously more hopeful.

On the surface the congress disposed of its business with reasonable dispatch and relative harmony. The catch phrase, in Lenin's absence, was "party unity," and few dared to challenge the collective will even though there was no attempt to prevent the free expression of opinion. Stalin, modesty personified, invoked Lenin's name with dignity and respect, avoiding the self-serving tributes that sprang so easily to the lips of Zinoviev and Kamenev. Posing as the humble disciple, he scrupulously avoided the kind of extravagant rhetoric that would call undue attention to himself or to his entrenched position in the party apparatus. The Secretariat had done its work well behind the scenes, and most of the delegates, if not beholden to Stalin, were unlikely to embarrass him with searching questions. Yet a speaker of Trotsky's skill and reputation, using the ammunition that Lenin had provided, could have captured the congress. He declined to do so, and the opportunity never recurred. Abiding by his understanding with Stalin, he confined his major address to economic problems and announced his solidarity with the party leadership. He even rebuked a supporter who complained that his services had not been fully utilized.

The nationalities question did arouse a heated discussion. The Georgian "nationalists" could hardly have anticipated success. Soundly defeated at a conference of the Georgian party shortly after Lenin's third attack, they could claim only two representatives at the congress. Their hope that Lenin's nationalities memorandum would be published and that Trotsky would take up the cause were disappointed by his continued silence, interrupted only by an insipid article on the problem in *Pravda* on March 20. It was left to Fotieva to resurrect Lenin's commentary. She wrote Kamenev about it, and a copy circulated among the members of the Central Committee. Its contents, if not the document itself, became known to nearly all the delegates. Stalin, as the principal speaker on the nationalities issue, gave a virtuoso performance: he too was an enemy of Great Russian chauvinism and a friend of national autonomy. And speaking of chauvinism, he cleverly interjected, perhaps the Georgian "deviators" opposed the Transcaucasian federation because their own national minorities—the Armenians, Ossetians, Tartars, etc.—might gain too much independence. Besides, "after two years of contention, the Mdivani group is a small handful, repeatedly ejected by the Party in Georgia itself."[21]

Trotsky, of course, kept his own counsel and avoided the sessions dealing with the nationalities question. Bukharin was the only party member of note to take up the Georgian case, though it was Khristian Rakovsky, the Ukrainian premier and an associate of Trotsky, who delivered the most freewheeling criticism of Stalin's policy. (Not surprisingly, he was shifted to a new post as Soviet envoy in London during the summer.) A resolution to weaken the representation of the Russian republic in relation to the other three republics in the constitutional framework of the U.S.S.R. was dismissed by Stalin as "administrative fetishism" and easily voted down.

Lenin had become convinced that the governmental and party machinery needed major repairs, but his last thoughts on the subject scarcely constituted a remedy for the leviathan of bureaucracy. The party leaders readily took up his suggestions, for they, no less than their ailing mentor, were anxious to array themselves on the side of righteousness and administrative efficiency against the baneful forces of incompetence and red tape. The Central Committee acquired thirteen new members, and the Central Control Commission, originally established as a check on party officials, was increased from seven to fifty and authorized to participate in plenary sessions of the Central Committee. Rabkrin, the target of Lenin's last published article, was merged with the Central Control Commission. Since experienced personnel could not be plucked directly from the factory bench, as Lenin, in a burst of utopian fantasy, had strongly implied, the Secretariat inevitably became the channel through which the appointments were made. Lenin's fight against bureaucracy ended with the strengthening of Stalin's hold on the party levers.

Lenin knew nothing—or at most very little—of the party congress or current affairs. After recovering consciousness he was frustrated and depressed by his inability to speak beyond an occasional monosyllable and sometimes lost his temper when his gestures were misunderstood. On those occasions he would shoo away the attending physicians, nurses, and orderlies. In the spring he was moved on a stretcher from his Kremlin apartment and taken to Gorki in an ambulance. During the summer he showed marked improvement, no longer bedridden and eventually able to walk with assistance. Krupskaya began the laborious process of speech therapy, and he tried to learn to write with his left hand, but progress was painfully slow. The available evidence indicates that his thinking capacity remained substantially intact and that his disability was physical (and to some extent, considering the circumstances, psychological). Nevertheless, the rumor spread, apparently in party circles, that he was a "gibbering idiot."

On October 18, suddenly feeling much better, Lenin insisted on a visit to Moscow. Accompanied by Krupskaya and Maria Ulyanova, among others, he was driven to the Kremlin and visited his office for the last time. The accounts of his trip vary in detail, and one indicates that he became upset when he could not find a document he was looking for. He stayed overnight in his apartment and allegedly visited an agricultural exhibit the next day. Returning to the Kremlin to pick up some books from his library, he was then driven back to Gorki. The press did not comment on the incident, nor did any party leaders, as far as is known, attempt to see him during his brief stay in Moscow.

Toward the end of the year Lenin's health showed occasional signs of deterioration, yet he attended a Christmas party and appeared to be in good spirits. Curiously, during the late summer and fall when he had been permitted a few visitors, chiefly local peasant or worker delegations, he saw none of the party notables except Bukharin. This may have been his personal preference, but probably Krupskaya, in consultation with the doctors, placed a ban on such meetings as potentially too disturbing.

On January 19, 1924, Lenin's vision apparently began to fail. He suffered a relapse the next day, and on the evening of the 21st he suffered another major stroke. With his body wracked by muscular spasms and his temperature mounting rapidly, he lost consciousness. At 6:50 P.M., with Krupskaya at his bedside holding his hand, Lenin died of a massive cerebral hemorrhage.

CHAPTER X

Leninism and the Lenin Cult

LENIN'S DEATH WAS A SHOCKING SURPRISE TO THE GENERAL PUBLIC, for the nature and severity of his illness had never been fully revealed. A spontaneous outpouring of grief, unprecedented in Russian history, swept the nation. The masses had known little but hardship under Communist rule, yet Lenin had already become something of a folk hero. To the politically unsophisticated he fell into the tradition of the "good Tsar" who fought for the people against their oppressors. But it would have been an uncommonly backward peasant who failed to associate him specifically with the land reform of 1917. In the eyes of party members and sympathizers throughout the world he underwent a process of instant canonization—a secular saint whose image, in tandem with that of Marx, was to survive unscathed amid the quarrels and vicissitudes of twentieth-century Communism. Even some of his enemies grudgingly acknowledged that the "Red dictator," however misguided, had remained uncorrupted by power and dedicated to his vision of a better society.

An autopsy was performed at Gorki on January 22 in the presence of ten physicians and the commissar for public health. It disclosed heavy sclerosis of the blood vessels in the brain, a condition so advanced that it seemed astonishing that Lenin had lived as long as he had. Despite the meticulous autopsy report, rumors circulated in Moscow that poison had somehow been involved in his death. But nothing specific found its way into print until many years later when Trotsky, from his exile in Mexico, suggested in a magazine article that Stalin may have poisoned Lenin. He elaborated the charge in a biography of Stalin, unfinished at the time of his assassination in 1940, that was published posthumously.[1] But the "evidence" is hardly more than speculation, although there may be substance to his account of a Politburo meeting near the end of February, 1923, at which Stalin is said to have informed his colleagues that Lenin had requested poison to end his suffering.

Lenin's brain was retained for research purposes on the theory that his intellectual capacity was so remarkable that physiological evidence would surely be disclosed by detailed examination. Such a hypothesis had a special appeal to the Soviet leaders, steeped as they were in the materialist philosophy of Marxism. A German expert was induced to head a special institute for the dissection and study, but his findings were inconclusive, and apart from propaganda releases the assumed correlation between genius and brain structure—a dubious proposition on the face of it—was never scientifically demonstrated.

Deceased party members, even the most notable, were usually cremated. Lenin's body was embalmed, a decision made at the highest party level over Krupskaya's objections. What better icon to legitimize the political succession and to bemuse the pious masses than the preservation of the outer shell of Lenin himself? After numerous delegations of party officials and workers paid their respects at Gorki, the remains were taken by special train to Moscow and displayed in the Hall of Columns of the House of Trade Unions, once a resplendent club for the tsarist nobility. Outside in the bitter cold long queues formed, and for four days and nights a seemingly endless procession of mourners filed past the bier in respectful and sometimes tearful silence. According to official figures, over 900,000 people obtained a glimpse of the dead leader, far more than those who saw him during his lifetime.

The opening session of the Congress of Soviets on January 26 was devoted to memorial speeches. Like the eulogies that filled the press, they tended to be banal and repetitious. Only two departed significantly from conventional party rhetoric: Krupskaya's tribute, brief and moving, and Stalin's, curiously reminiscent of the Orthodox litany, which contained a repeated "vow" to carry forward Lenin's "commandments." Afterwards identified as "Stalin's oath," the speech gained a certain notoriety, partly for its psychological astuteness but mainly because of the subsequent fame of the speaker. The congress resolved, obviously in response to decisions already made by the troika, to have Lenin's works published in the major languages, a popular version as well as a complete scholarly edition; to rename the former capital

Leningrad; and to preserve Lenin's body in a mausoleum to be built in Red Square near the Kremlin wall. Krupskaya, knowing her husband's distaste for ceremonial splendor, protested in vain, although *Pravda* did print her appeal that the nation's grief should not take the form of "external reverence" for Lenin's person.

The next morning, a Sunday, the coffin was removed to a temporary platform in Red Square, and numerous delegations, some from the far reaches of the Soviet Union, marched past in tribute. More speeches were heard—the less exalted now had their opportunity—and at four in the afternoon artillery salvoes and factory whistles delivered a prolonged and noisy farewell salute as the party leaders carried the coffin into a temporary wooden tomb. Among Lenin's close associates only Trotsky was missing. He had been en route to the warmer climate of the Black Sea when informed of Lenin's death, and according to his autobiography Stalin's telegram deceived him about the date of the funeral and urged him to continue his journey since he could not return in time. His absence, while embarrassing to his followers, had little bearing on his later political fortunes (contrary to journalistic accounts that gained currency in the West).

The original embalming method proved unsatisfactory, and specialists allegedly devised a new chemical process to preserve the corpse indefinitely. A more durable tomb was opened to the public on August 1, 1924. Six years later it was replaced by an elaborate mausoleum of granite and porphyry. From the beginning the Communist shrine on Red Square proved to be immensely popular, a mecca for tourists and pilgrims alike. The irony of its sponsorship by a state proclaiming atheism as its official doctrine concealed a shrewd compromise with the realities of Russian backwardness and the psychology of its people.

Rumors persisted among skeptics that Lenin's "body" was nothing but a wax figure. When similar reports were published abroad in the 1930s, a number of foreigners were invited to witness the opening of the hermetically sealed glass case. The chief embalming chemist "tweaked Lenin's nose and turned his head to the right and left," convincing at least one observer that "it was not wax."[2] In 1941, with the German attack on the Soviet Union, the body was transported to Kuibyshev (originally Samara) for safekeeping and returned to the mausoleum in 1945.

Again rumors circulated that it was not really Lenin's body, and there were those who claimed that it had improved in appearance, indicating further work by embalmers, cosmetologists, or both.

With Stalin's death in 1953—the funeral rites were as lavish as those for Lenin—the mausoleum lost its exclusivity when Stalin's embalmed remains were placed beside those of Lenin. The interloper's tenure was relatively brief, however, for in 1961, in response to attacks on Stalin's "cult of personality," the body was removed and reburied in a modest plot near the Kremlin wall. The Twenty-Second Party Congress had denounced as "blasphemy" the continued intimacy of the two even in death. An Old Bolshevik, in a fascinating example of necromancy, told the delegates to "stormy prolonged applause" that she had "asked Ilyich for advice, and it was as if he stood before me alive and said: 'I do not like being next to Stalin, who inflicted so much harm on the party.' "[3]

The fate of Lenin's Testament, the leader's most important legacy to the party (aside from the Leninist mystique itself), adds to the impression that Stalin was extraordinarily fortunate to survive the years 1923–24 with his political career intact. Krupskaya sent the document to Kamenev with a note indicating Lenin's wish that his remarks be read to the next party congress after his death. On May 22, 1924, on the eve of the Thirteenth Congress, a Central Committee meeting (including other key party members) heard the Testament. It was particularly embarrassing to Stalin, and all the participants seemed to have been ill at ease. Zinoviev, seconded by Kamenev, came to the rescue of the general secretary, convinced that Trotsky was the foremost pretender to the party leadership. The burden of their argument —that Lenin's fears had proved ill-founded—persuaded a majority of those present, and by a vote of thirty to ten it was decided to restrict the text to the heads of delegations attending the congress. A week or so later Stalin formally submitted his resignation as party secretary to the Central Committee. As he had no doubt anticipated, it was rejected—and by a unanimous vote.

Krupskaya, while never a high-ranking party member, derived great prestige and no little moral authority by the mere fact of being Lenin's widow. To Stalin she remained an irritating reminder of his troubles with Lenin, and even at the peak of his power he never dared attack her publicly. She briefly joined the anti-Stalinist opposition but defected in the fall of 1926, ostensibly for the sake of party unity. In 1930 she spoke in support of Bukharin and Rykov (then leaders of the Right opposition) at a district party conference. Thereafter, on Stalin's instructions, she was kept under close surveillance. Nikita Khrushchev recalled her as a "broken old woman" whom "people avoided like the plague."[4] Stalin went out of his way to attack her in outrageous terms when among his cronies and professed doubt that she was really Lenin's widow. He supposedly threatened to name another woman, a respected party member, to the "official" position, a report that bears a striking resemblance to Stalin's notorious phone call to Krupskaya in 1923 in which he is said to have warned: "If you don't behave yourself we'll get another widow for Lenin."[5] She died in 1939, still a revered figure as far as the general public was concerned.

Stalin's pose as a faithful and modest disciple of the great Lenin never faltered even when it was no longer politically necessary (though no doubt still expedient). The other leaders, notably Zinoviev and Trotsky, saw no need for dissimulation. While always respectful of the developing Lenin cult, they conveyed an impression of close collaboration rather than discipleship. Zinoviev was indefatigable as a commemorative writer and speaker, and he could truthfully claim greater intimacy with Lenin during the years immediately preceding the Bolshevik Revolution than anyone else. Trotsky, though a latecomer to the party fold, made his own contribution to Leniniana in the early summer of 1924 with a brief memoir written in a tone of deferential but affectionate intimacy (while conveniently ignoring the embarrassing years of their estrangement) that proved offensive to his rivals.

But Stalin's ultimate triumph in the struggle for power was only incidentally related to the political gamesmanship that sought to exploit the dead leader's prestige. His control of the party machinery was considerably enhanced by the so-called "Lenin enrollment" of 1924 in which the party was swamped with young and inexperienced recruits, mostly "workers from the bench." Lenin had attempted in his last years to rid the party of careerists and opportunists who had crept in during the expansion dictated by the civil war emergency. He had tended to think in terms of quality, not quantity, and the decision to lower the barriers once more—over 200,000 new members were admitted and others purged—was questionable by the standards of Leninist orthodoxy. However, the old elitist concept of the party as an exclusive fraternity of devoted revolutionaries was no longer appropriate to its altered status: administrative talent had replaced conspiratorial skill as the prime requisite of the model Communist. Yet Lenin's confidence in the proletariat and his corresponding distrust of intellectuals was supported by the preference displayed for industrial workers, who would, presumably because of the purity of their class origin, bring nothing but dedicated virtue to the party. But what agency other than Stalin's apparatus was equipped to deal with this massive transfusion of new party blood?

When, in the late twenties, Stalin had consolidated his position as dictator, the cult of Lenin showed no obvious signs of diminution. Gradually, nevertheless, Lenin was converted into an abstract godhead whose principles were inviolable and whose deeds were mighty, but the man himself became lost in pious legend, and his ideology served only to add luster to the existing regime. A secret Politburo decision of August, 1938, prohibited new publications about him and authorized the destruction of numerous memoirs already in print. Outwardly the loyal and unassuming Leninist he had always been, Stalin in reality superseded the party's founder, not only in the mechanics of power and the authority of his personal rule but also in the ritual and iconography of "sainthood" and in the loathsome adulation that surrounded his person.

The "de-Stalinization" that began so sensationally with Khrushchev's famous speech to the Twentieth Party Congress in 1956 led to a refurbishing of the Lenin cult. The party under Stalin was said to have departed from "Leninist norms." Khrushchev's abrupt fall from grace in 1964 left the new oligarchy in a quandary. If a tyrant (Stalin) and a bungler (Khrushchev) had presided over the party and the state for the past forty years, even the most politically innocent citizen might begin to question the quality of Soviet leadership. And there were always malcontents who would be tempted to probe more deeply into the nature of Soviet society. Again the sacred name proved a useful crutch, a certificate of respectability for the status quo that defied the most daring iconoclast. The production of Leniniana, already a major industry under Stalin until the 1938 decree (though singularly innocuous and carefully regulated) had been renovated under Khrushchev and attained new records under Leonid Brezhnev. But the hagiographic tradition remained intact, and the few grains of authenticity were buried in the chaff of sanctified dogma and semifictional "memoirs."

The apotheosis of the Lenin cult came in 1970 with the centennial celebration of his birth. The dedication of new monuments and museums, the publication of essays, poems, and books, the minting of a jubilee coin, and the variety of commemorative celebrations held throughout the Soviet Union and in many foreign countries, Communist and non-Communist, testified to the durability of his image and to the respect and affection in which his memory was held. But simplicity and spontaneity, the very qualities that Lenin would have appreciated, were lost in the elaborate ritual and stereotyped rhetoric of the formal ceremonies. The climactic tribute took place at the Kremlin's Palace of Congresses on April 21 in a joint session of the Central Committee and the Supreme Soviet, together with representatives of the peoples within the Soviet Union as well as Communist delegations from abroad. Brezhnev delivered the keynote address, a dull and hackneyed recital of Lenin's principles and achievements that nearly everyone present must have heard or read a hundred times before. Nor did the notables who followed him to the speaker's rostrum improve upon it except in the comparative brevity of their remarks. Political eulogies, even when the recipient is worthy and the homage is sincere, seldom rise above the commonplace, and on this occasion the spokesmen of official Communism could contrive nothing more than the same tired clichés to honor their founding father.

Like Marx before him, Lenin died while his "system" was still reasonably flexible and before it had acquired the authority of an institutionalized credo. That he would have endorsed the acts—or even the principles—of those who so freely invoked his name seems more than doubtful. And he would most certainly have repudiated the personal glorification that tended to demean his achievements. "During the lifetime of great revolutionaries," he had written in *State and Revolution,* the oppressing classes reacted with "savage fury" and "unscrupulous campaigns of lies and slander." Upon their death "attempts are made to convert them into harmless icons, to canonize them, so to speak, and to allow the glorification of their *names* for the 'consolation' of the oppressed classes with the object of duping them, while at the same time cutting away the substance of the revolutionary theory, blunting its revolutionary edge and vulgarizing it."[6]

However widely Stalin departed from Leninist orthodoxy during the years of his dictatorship, it is undeniably true that he would never have been in a position to seize power without Lenin's patronage. Nor could he have used the party as a pliable instrument of his personal rule had not Lenin founded Bolshevism and shaped it in his own image. Yet the facile assumption of Western commentators that Stalinism was simply Leninism writ large, a logical and even inevitable development in the evolution of the party, is to embrace a theory of historical determinism of the crudest sort. The personal factor, as intangible and unsatisfactory as it may be in the complex mosaic of historical causation, must be given major if not decisive importance. Trotsky was scarcely the hard-bitten Bolshevik cast in the Leninist mold, but he nevertheless became Lenin's hesitant choice as successor (insofar as anyone was so designated), and he frittered away his opportunity with the fatal irresolution of a Russian Hamlet. Even assuming the worst about Stalin—and Lenin was not quite prepared to make that irrevocable assumption—the ailing leader would have been a clairvoyant of unparalleled sagacity had he anticipated that the plebeian general secretary would one day emerge as a paranoid tyrant. Whatever its ambiguous legacy, Leninism cannot be charged with direct responsibility for Stalinism and its unique brand of totalitarian Communism.

The original doctrine has proved amorphous enough to include a spectacular and varied array of "Leninists" from Tito to Mao, and Marxism-Leninism has become an incantation, if not a working program, for all manner of "leftists" espousing a revolutionary creed. And debased though it may be by the ideological and personal mediocrity of many self-proclaimed disciples, Leninism seems assured of a special mystique in those "backward" countries that have never had the kind of industrial capitalism or bourgeois social order described in classical Marxism. Modernization and material equality with the "advanced" nations has become the goal of assorted national "socialists" whose dedication to Leninism is in many cases more ritualistic than actual. Lenin's historic legacy has thus been to bridge the doctrinal chasm between Western-oriented Marxism and an "Asiatic" style of revolutionary protest in which personal freedom is subordinated to economic progress and social justice.

In attempting to rescue the "real" Lenin from the ravages of historical myth mongering and the demands of political orthodoxy, a number of judgments about his personal qualities can be made. He was on the whole a likable human being, a statement that would be inappropriate for most individuals who have wielded power on a comparable scale. Genuinely modest, thoughtful to friends and associates, devoid of personal ambition, and indifferent to material gain or the pleasures of the flesh, he would seem a paragon of virtue if one were to divorce his private life from his political career. Nor did he acquire the petty vices and bad habits that to most people become a normal part of everyday life. Neat, precise, and punctual, he neither smoked nor drank, and his only known—or suspected—departure from marital fidelity was his "romance" with Inessa Armand. One might well argue that asceticism combined with enormous will power were among those traits that enabled him—essentially a decent and humane man—to pursue a political course that involved not only selflessness and dedication but ruthlessness and moral insensitivity when the occasion seemed to demand it.

Lenin's fondness for cats provides a fleeting glimpse into another facet of his personality. Subtle, dignified, and haughtily independent, the feline tends to be admired by intellectuals and "inner-directed" types and disliked by those with tender egoes and other manifestations of psychological immaturity. Politicians, including dictators, can more readily identify with dogs (a sociable animal and excellent ego boosters). Lenin's preference for cats is perhaps unique among the political luminaries of the modern world.

Lenin's emotional life is effectively concealed by the paucity of available knowledge. But it is entirely possible that Soviet archives contain nuggets of information that will some day furnish important clues—and perhaps new insights—about his personal life and motivations. He had a sense of humor and could laugh at himself, one indicator of a reasonably healthy psyche. Yet he suffered intermittently with depression and nervous tension, accompanied by headaches and insomnia, throughout his mature life. Although a physical basis for his ailments cannot be ruled out, particularly in view of his ultimately fatal disease, these are typical psychosomatic symptoms. One can only speculate about the psychological causes, presumably rooted in his childhood, that contributed to his recurring illness. If he was not always the strong and confident personality of Soviet legend, neither was he a neurasthenic, an emotional cripple whose revolutionary career became an outlet for subliminal drives and neurotic impulses. He displayed none of the egocentricity that can be considered almost normal behavior for celebrities, political and otherwise. Nor did he seem to relish power for its own sake, thus avoiding the "corruption" that Lord Acton's famous maxim warned against. His "charisma," such as it was, depended upon force of intellect and solid political achievement, not upon a gift for demagogy or other manifestations of a psychopathic personality.

Lenin was a political creature par excellence. He seldom had the time or inclination, especially after 1917, to devote to literature and the arts—or indeed any cultural activity unrelated to politics or revolutionary ideology. He was not the type of intellectual who pursues knowledge for its own sake. Disinterested scholarship was as alien to his temperament as the investigation of theology or metaphysics for personal enlightenment, although he was a prodigious researcher and had studied philosophy to confound the critics of materialism. He remained oblivious to the new currents in psychology, notably the Freudian school, but it would be unfair to reproach him for ignorance or intellectual timidity in a field so remote from his experience and whose wider implications were disregarded even by professional psychologists. Nevertheless, his rationalistic view of human nature—a view that derived from the eighteenth-century Enlightenment and which he shared with Marx—was surprisingly ingenuous, a serious flaw in his "system" that he implicitly recognized by ultimately retreating from the utopianism of *State and Revolution.*

Lenin was not dogmatic about the role of the state as the guardian of literary and esthetic standards. The early 1920s, compared to the cultural obscurantism of the Stalin era, was a period of freedom and experimentation for the creative intelligentsia—always provided that "counterrevolutionary" sentiments were not in evidence. Lenin's personal tastes were rather conventional, and he believed that literature and the arts should be accessible to the masses: "Art belongs to the people. It must have its deepest roots in the broad mass of workers. It must be understood and loved by them. It must be rooted in and grow with their feelings, thoughts and desires. It must arouse and develop the artist in them."[7] Such opinions, soon to become indistinguishable from standard party cant, were made without political malice, and Lenin conferred a fair measure of cultural autonomy on his commissar for education, Lunacharsky, whose domain encompassed a wide spectrum of intellectual and esthetic activity. But his misgivings about avant-garde intellectuals and their outlandish creations were never far below the surface. "I cannot value the works of expressionism, futurism, cubism, and other isms as the highest expressions of artistic genius," he complained. "I don't understand them. They give me no pleasure."[8] He was not above peevish comments and an occasional outburst. In 1921, for example, he reproached Lunacharsky for allowing 5,000 copies of Vladimir Mayakovsky's poem *150,000,000* to be published. "It's rubbish, ridiculous, arrant nonsense and pretentiousness," he wrote. "I think we should print only 1 in 10 of such things, and *no more than 1,500 copies* for libraries and cranks."[9]

Lenin spoke of himself, with a kind of wry irony, as a "gloomy ascetic." His self-appraisal was not far wrong, for his life style was austere and impeccably "bourgeois." On questions of marriage, the family, and sexual morality, as in art and literature, he was almost invariably conservative. To many Communists, "free love" had become a symbol of emancipation from bourgeois morality: the satisfaction of the sexual appetite should be as simple as drinking a glass of water. But Lenin emphatically rejected the theory. "Will the normal man in normal circumstances," he asked rhetorically, "lie down in the gutter and drink out of a puddle, or out of a glass with a rim greasy from many lips?" A puritan among Communists, he believed in "healthy bodies" and "healthy minds," presumably to be acquired through the "self-control" and "self-discipline" that he had practiced throughout his life.[10] On the other hand, he enthusiastically supported equality for women, including liberalized abortion and easy divorce, an attitude that prompted "progressive" social legislation until Stalin reversed the trend in the 1930s.

Lenin's reputation obviously rests upon other criteria than his character and personality, however estimable. Nor does it derive from his views on nonpolitical subjects, though "politics," even in the early years of Soviet Russia, encompassed a far wider range of activity than in any other state. While almost everyone has been willing to concede Lenin's genius as a revolutionary leader, not all have been equally impressed with his record as a statesman. Inevitably the problems of the professional revolutionary multiply in a dramatic progression once he has obtained political power. Few have been privileged to play both roles. Only Stalin and Mao Tse-tung, among Communist rulers, have done so on an equivalent scale, and neither seems likely to challenge Lenin regarding the quality of their statesmanship (though both, paradoxically, presided over a more profound economic and social transformation than did Lenin during the short period of his ascendancy). Of course, it may be legitimately argued that no one could have governed Russia with any great degree of success once the tsarist regime was swept away. However, that does not absolve Lenin from criticism, not necessarily for specific errors of judgment (e.g., the Red Army's march into Poland or the elevation of Stalin to a commanding position in the party) but for the direction in which he led the Soviet republic in its infancy.

As the creator of the world's first Communist state, Lenin deliberately opted for a one-party dictatorship and renounced the essence of parliamentary democracy as an empty fraud. True, he was soon faced with a bloody civil war that at least partially justified his reliance upon arbitrary methods of rule. But the "siege" was eventually lifted with no modification of the strict political regimen that he had originally levied, though he did allow a strategic retreat in the economic sector. Indeed, when it would appear to have been advisable—certainly statesmanlike—to make a few gestures toward political reconciliation, he insisted on further persecution of the Mensheviks and virtually ended intra-party democracy with the ban on factionalism in 1921. Communism, well before the rigors of Stalinism, therefore became associated with an authoritarian if not monolithic party. Had Lenin attained a normal life span there is every possibility that some variety of "socialist humanism" would have ameliorated the party dictatorship. Communism instead acquired the harsh and tyrannical image associated with Stalin and has never managed to regain the Leninist ideal—admittedly an ambiguous legacy—despite the constant invocation of his name.

The scorn that Lenin heaped upon "bourgeois democracy," while not entirely misplaced (the "free" market, private profit, and the business cycle have been its economic corollaries) seems a half century later an inappropriate response to a political system, however imperfect, that has tended to safeguard civil liberties and free intellectual inquiry. Such amenities have been notably lacking in those nations that have subscribed to Marxist-Leninist ideology, and some have plausibly maintained that political repression is the inevitable price that must be paid for material progress in a predominantly agrarian society. It is well to be reminded that the "early" Lenin—vintage 1905—was by no means opposed to formal democracy. "Whoever wants to approach socialism by any other path than that of political democracy," he warned prophetically, "will inevitably arrive at the most absurd and reactionary conclusions, both in the economic and political sense."[11]

Despite the anti-democratic legacy of Leninism, the man himself, perhaps because of his common core of humanity and his personal selflessness, does not convey an image of autocratic rule. The more recent memory of Hitler and Stalin, by way of comparison, tends to confer an aura of benignity upon Lenin that may not be entirely deserved. But in popular legend, particularly in the "socialist" and "nonaligned" world, his name continues to serve an important function as Communism's better conscience: the symbol of a doctrine and an ideal, unfortunately perverted in practice, that claims for its devotees a secular and material rather than a supernatural solution to the problems of human existence.

Reference Notes

CHAPTER I

1. V. I. Lenin, *Polnoe sobranie sochineny* (5th ed., Moscow, 1958–65),
XXX, 327–28. Unless otherwise indicated, all citations to Lenin's works
refer to this edition, with the notation "Lenin" followed by the appropriate volume and page number.

2. *Ibid.*, XLIX, 340.

3. N. N. Krupskaya, *Reminiscences of Lenin* (Moscow, 1959), p. 338.

4. Maxim Gorky, *Days With Lenin* (New York, 1932), p. 52.

5. Z. A. B. Zeman (ed.), *Germany and the Revolution in Russia*
(London, 1958). See also Werner Hahlweg (ed.), *Lenins Rückkehr
nach Russland 1917* (Leiden, 1957).

6. Z. A. B. Zeman and W. B. Scharlau, *Merchant of Revolution*
(London, 1965), p. 217.

7. Michael Futrell, *Northern Underground* (London, 1963), p. 156.

CHAPTER II

1. P. N. Pospelov and others, *Vladimir Ilyich Lenin: A Biography*
(Moscow, 1965), p. 22.

2. *Ibid.*, p. 24.

3. Nikolay Valentinov, *Encounters With Lenin* (London, 1968), p. 66.

4. Nikolai Valentinov, *The Early Years of Lenin* (Ann Arbor, Mich.,
1969), p. 173.

5. *Ibid.*, p. 149.

6. Krupskaya, p. 13.

7. P. A. Berlin, V. S. Voitinsky, and B. I. Nikolayevsky (eds.), *Perepiska Plekhanova i P. B. Akselroda* (Moscow, 1925), I, 269–71.

8. Gorky, p. 54.

9. Lenin, II, 13.

10. Yu. Martov, *Zapiski sotsial-demokrata* (Moscow, 1924), p. 294.

11. Elizabeth Hill and Doris Mudie (eds.), *The Letters of Lenin*
(New York, 1937), p. 21.

12. *Novy mir*, No. 6 (June 1963), p. 175.

13. Lenin, LV, 80.

14. *Ibid.*, pp. 107–08.

15. *Ibid.*, p. 176.

CHAPTER III

1. Lenin, IV, 331.
2. Text of the memorandum, *ibid.*, pp. 322–52.
3. *Perepiska Plekhanova i Akselroda,* II, 146.
4. Leon Trotsky, *Lenin: Notes for a Biographer* (New York, 1971), p. 40.
5. Lenin, IV, 373 and 376.
6. Krupskaya, p. 71.
7. Leon Trotsky, *My Life* (New York, 1930), p. 143; Trotsky, *Lenin,* p. 34.
8. Lenin, XLVI, 186.
9. *Leninsky sbornik* (Moscow, 1924–45), III, 430.
10. Trotsky, *My Life,* p. 163; Trotsky, *Lenin,* p. 69.
11. G. V. Plekhanov, *Sochinenia* (2nd ed.; Moscow, 1923–27), XIII, 91.
12. Valentinov, *Encounters With Lenin,* p. 114.
13. *Leninsky sbornik,* X, 353.
14. See Vadim Medish, "Lenin and Japanese Money," *Russian Review,* XXIV (April 1965), 165–76.

CHAPTER IV

1. Lenin, IX, 211.
2. *Ibid.,* XLVII, 52.
3. *Ibid.,* XII, 61 and 63.
4. Pospelov, p. 127, summarizes his activities.
5. Lenin, XIII, 371 and 376.
6. *Ibid.,* XII, 285.
7. *Ibid.,* XIV, 318.
8. *Ibid.,* XV, 296 and 297–98.
9. See Arthur P. Dudden and Theodore H. von Laue, "The RSDLP and Joseph Fels: A Study in Intercultural Contact," *American Historical Review,* LXI (October 1955), 21–47.
10. Krupskaya, pp. 157–58.
11. *Ibid.,* p. 161.
12. *Ibid.,* p. 162.

CHAPTER V

1. Lenin, XLVII, 137.
2. *Ibid.,* p. 142.
3. *Ibid.,* pp. 143 and 148.
4. Leonard Schapiro, *The Communist Party of the Soviet Union* (2nd ed.; New York, 1971), pp. 111–12.

5. Bertram D. Wolfe, *Three Who Made a Revolution* (Boston, 1955), p. 512. On Bogdanov, see S. V. Utechin's article in Leopold Labedz (ed.), *Revisionism: Essays on the History of Marxist Ideas* (London, 1962), and Dietrich Grille, *Lenins Rivale: Bogdanov und seine Philosophie* (Cologne, 1966).

6. Lenin, XLVII, 276.

7. See Ralph Carter Elwood, "Lenin and the Social Democratic Schools for Underground Party Workers, 1909–11," *Political Science Quarterly*, LXXXI (September 1966), 370–91.

8. See Bertram D. Wolfe, "Lenin and Inessa Armand," *Slavic Review*, XXII (March 1963), 96–114.

9. Lenin, XLVIII, 69.

10. Krupskaya, p. 233.

11. Lenin, LV, 329 and 354.

12. *Ibid.*, p. 347.

13. *Ibid.*, XLVIII, 305 and 316.

14. *Ibid.*, XXV, 400.

15. *Ibid.*, XLVIII, 155.

16. Krupskaya, p. 290.

17. *Ibid.*, XXVI, 6.

18. *Ibid.*, pp. 168 and 174.

19. *Ibid.*, XLIX, 233 and 236.

20. Alfred Erich Senn, *The Russian Revolution in Switzerland, 1914–1917* (Madison, Wis., 1971), p. 96.

21. Olga Hess Gankin and H. H. Fisher, *The Bolsheviks and the World War* (Stanford, Calif., 1940), p. 419.

22. Lenin, XXVII, 521.

CHAPTER VI

1. Nikolai Sukhanov, *Zapiski o revolyutsii* (Berlin, St. Petersburg, and Moscow, 1922–23), III, 14–15.

2. *Ibid.*, p. 40.

3. Lenin, XXXI, 362.

4. *Ibid.*, XXXII, 267.

5. *Ibid.*, p. 327.

6. *Ibid.*, p. 360.

7. Documents and related bibliographical references may be found in Robert Paul Browder and Alexander F. Kerensky (eds.), *The Russian Provisional Government, 1917* (Stanford, Calif., 1961), III, 1364–82. See also George Katkov, *Russia 1917: The February Revolution* (New York, 1967), especially pp. 109–15, and the same author's article in Richard Pipes (ed.), *Revolutionary Russia* (Garden City, N.Y., 1969), pp. 80–122.

8. For a "revisionist" view see Rodney Barfield, "Lenin's Utopianism: *State and Revolution*," *Slavic Review*, XXX (March 1971), 45–56.

9. W. S. Woytinsky, *Stormy Passage* (New York, 1961), p. 314.

10. Lenin, XXXIV, 17 and 69.

11. A. F. Kerensky, *The Prelude to Bolshevism* (London, 1919), p. 19.

12. Lenin, XXXIV, 241.

13. *Proletarskaya revolyutsia,* No. 10 (October 1922), p. 319.

14. Lenin, XXXIV, 282.

15. Leon Trotsky, *The History of the Russian Revolution* (New York, 1936), III, 148.

16. *Ibid.,* p. 151.

17. Lenin, XXXIV, 435–36.

18. Trotsky, *My Life,* p. 337; Trotsky, *Lenin,* p. 98.

19. *Kommunist,* No. 1 (January 1957), p. 43.

CHAPTER VII

1. Trotsky, *My Life,* p. 338; Trotsky, *Lenin,* p. 119.

2. John Reed, *Ten Days That Shook the World* (New York, 1935), pp. 125–26.

3. Lenin, XXXV, 27.

4. Albert Rhys Williams, *Lenin: The Man and His Work* (New York, 1919), pp. 53–54.

5. Lenin, XXXVI, 174.

6. *Ibid.,* XXXV, 241–42.

7. *Ibid.,* XL, 10.

8. Trotsky, *My Life,* pp. 381–82.

9. M. A. Savelyeva (ed.), *Protokoly tsentralnovo Komiteta RSDRP, avgust 1917–fevral 1918* (Moscow, 1929), p. 246.

10. Vlad. Bonch-Bruyevich, *Na boevykh postakh fevralskoi i oktyabrskoi revolyutsii* (Moscow, 1931), p. 260.

11. Lenin, XXXVI, 215.

12. Trotsky, *Lenin,* p. 123.

13. Lenin, XXXVII, 359.

14. *Ibid.,* L, 106.

15. P. Malkov, *Reminiscences of a Kremlin Commandant* (Moscow, n.d.[c. 1964]), pp. 187 and 189.

16. Lenin, L, 182; XXXVII, 242, 244, and 287.

17. *Ibid.,* p. 304.

CHAPTER VIII

1. L. Fotieva, *Pages From Lenin's Life* (Moscow, 1960), p. 34.

2. Jan M. Meijer (ed.), *The Trotsky Papers, 1917–1922* (The Hague, 1964), I, 258–61.

3. *Ibid.*, pp. 482–83.

4. Lenin, XXXIX, 303.

5. *Ibid.*, XXXVII, 490.

6. Angelica Balabanoff, *My Life as a Rebel* (New York, 1938), pp. 175 and 223.

7. Lenin, XXXVIII, 260.

8. *Ibid.*, p. 321.

9. *Ibid.*, L, 310.

10. *Ibid.*, p. 354.

11. *Ibid.*, XL, 131.

12. *Ibid.*, L, 182; LI, 71.

13. *Ibid.*, XXXVIII, 139.

14. *Ibid.*, XL, 145, 161, and 245–46.

15. *Ibid.*, XLI, 38 and 42.

16. Victor Serge, *Memoirs of a Revolutionary* (London, 1963), p. 108.

17. Angelica Balabanoff, *Impressions of Lenin* (Ann Arbor, Mich., 1964), p. 111.

18. Bonch-Bruyevich, p. 275.

19. Lenin, XLI, 329.

20. *Ibid.*, p. 296.

21. *Ibid.*, LII, 76.

22. *Ibid.*, XLII, 202, 208, 226, and 234.

CHAPTER IX

1. Marx-Lenin Institute, *Desyaty sezd RKP(b), mart 1921 goda: stenografichesky otchet* (Moscow, 1963), p. 34.

2. Serge, p. 131.

3. Lenin, XLIII, 129.

4. *Ibid.*, XLIV, 75.

5. *Ibid.*, XLIII, 16–17.

6. Clara Zetkin, *Reminiscences of Lenin* (New York, 1934), p. 28.

7. V. N. Rozanov in *Vospominania o Vladimir Ilyche Lenine* (Moscow, 1956–60), II, 344.

8. J. V. Stalin, *Works* (Moscow, 1953–55), V, 137–38.

9. Alfred Rosmer, *Moscou sous Lénine* (Paris, 1953), p. 231.

10. Louis Fischer, *The Life of Lenin* (New York, 1964), p. 619.

11. Lenin, LIV, 327–28; Trotsky, *My Life*, p. 481.

12. Lenin, XLV, 211; Leon Trotsky, *The Stalin School of Falsification* (New York, 1937), pp. 66–67.

13. Lenin, XLV, 214.

14. *Ibid.*, LIV, 674–75.

15. These documents (Dec. 23, 1922–Jan. 6, 1923) may be found in Lenin, XLV, 343–77.

16. *Ibid.*, pp. 389–406.

17. *Ibid.*, LIV, 329; Trotsky, *My Life,* p. 483.

18. Lenin, LIV, 329–30.

19. Trotsky, *My Life,* p. 482.

20. *Ibid.,* p. 486.

21. Stalin, *Works,* V, 262.

CHAPTER X

1. Leon Trotsky, *Stalin* (new ed., New York, 1967), pp. 376–82.

2. Fischer, p. 675.

3. Charlotte Saikowski and Leo Gruliow (eds.), *Current Soviet Policies IV: The Documentary Record of the 22nd Congress of the Communist Party of the Soviet Union* (New York, 1962), p. 216.

4. *Khrushchev Remembers,* with an introduction by Edward Crankshaw (Boston, 1970), p. 45.

5. Harrison Salisbury (ed.), *The Soviet Union* (New York, 1967), p. 19.

6. Lenin, XXXIII, 5.

7. Zetkin, p. 13.

8. *Ibid.,* pp. 12–13.

9. Lenin, LII, 179.

10. Zetkin, pp. 49–51.

11. Lenin, XI, 16.

Bibliography

1. Lenin's Work

The most complete bibliography is that provided by the Institute of Marxism-Leninism: *Khronologichesky ukazatel proizvedeny V. I. Lenina* [Chronological Index to the Works of V. I. Lenin] (2 vols.; Moscow, 1959–62). A supplemental title index was published in 1963.

Five editions of Lenin's works have appeared under Soviet auspices. The most complete, while not as comprehensive as it purports to be, is the fifth: *Polnoe sobranie sochineny* [Complete Collected Works] (55 vols.; Moscow, 1958–65). All citations in the reference notes are to this edition, although the annotations and other editorial matter are not up to the standard set by the relatively brief second and third editions, which were published before historical truth became the handmaiden of party ideology. The most complete English edition (*Collected Works* [40 vols.; Moscow, 1960–68]) is based on the fourth Russian edition, with some material from the fifth. The translation is much superior to previous attempts. *Leninsky sbornik* [Lenin Miscellany] (35 vols.; Moscow, 1924–45) is a compilation of less significant Leniniana, most of it incorporated in the fifth edition.

There are many editions of Lenin's selected works in all major languages. Publications in English within recent years include *Selected Works* (3 vols.; New York, 1967), sponsored by the American Communist Party and drawn from the 40-volume English edition; James E. Connor (ed.), *On Politics and Revolution* (New York, 1968); Stefan T. Possony (ed.), *The Lenin Reader* (Chicago, 1966); and Henry M. Christman (ed.), *The Essential Works of Lenin* (New York, 1966), a Bantam paperback. Separate editions of the Leninist "classics," notably *What Is to Be Done?*, *Imperialism*, and *State and Revolution* are also widely available.

2. Works about Lenin

The biographies are too numerous to mention individually. Those written more than two decades ago tend toward factual obsolescence because of the publication of new material. The best work has been produced in the West, for hagiography rather than scholarship continues to dominate the Soviet approach to Lenin. For bibliographic appraisals, see Walter Laqueur's essay in his *The Fate of the Revolution* (London, 1967) and Robert D. Warth, "Lenin: The Western Image Forty Years After," *Antioch Review*, XXIV (Winter 1964–65).

There is nothing approaching a "definitive" biography of Lenin. The most satisfactory is incorporated in Adam Ulam's *The Bolsheviks* (New York, 1965), a lively and sophisticated work whose content is conveyed more accurately by the title of the London edition, *Lenin and the Bolsheviks*. A scholarly synthesis crammed with interpretive analysis (and perhaps a bit too opinionated), it is critical but not unsympathetic toward its protagonist. Louis Fischer's *The Life of Lenin* (New York, 1964) presents more detail than Ulam but is uneven in style and unduly erratic in organization. It emphasizes Soviet diplomacy and the period of Lenin's rule. Stefan T. Possony's *Lenin: The Compulsive Revolutionary* (2nd ed.; London, 1965) is unrelievedly hostile in tone, stressing his conspiratorial career and his alleged ties with Germany, though he is not specifically accused of being a German "agent." David Shub's *Lenin: A Biography* (Harmondsworth, Eng., 1966), a Pelican paperback, is also basically hostile (the author was a Menshevik) but written with reasonable restraint. Journalistic in style and content, it is nevertheless conscientiously researched even if some of the sources used are of dubious authenticity. Robert Payne's *The Life and Death of Lenin* (New York, 1964) is intended for an undiscriminating popular audience. It is entertaining, superficial, and unreliable.

An intriguing but not always convincing psychological biography has been attempted in E. Victor Wolfenstein's *The Revolutionary Personality: Lenin, Trotsky, Gandhi* (Princeton, N.J., 1967). Two unfinished biographies may be noted: Isaac Deutscher, *Lenin's Childhood* (New York, 1970), a promising fragment of what was intended to be a major life of Lenin before the author's untimely death, and Leon Trotsky's *The Young Lenin* (New York, 1972), written (in the 1930s) with characteristic verve and for many years accessible only in a French edition. The encomiums written in the Soviet Union are virtually useless as serious scholarship. The latest and most elaborate is that of P. N. Pospelov and others, *Vladimir Ilych Lenin: A Biography* (Moscow, 1965).

Among older works of merit, the relevant chapters of Bertram D. Wolfe's *Three Who Made a Revolution* (Boston, 1955) deal perceptively and in considerable detail with Lenin's career up to 1914. Gerard Walter's *Lénine* (Paris, 1950) is a readable narrative by an admirer. Nina Gourfinkel's *Lenin* (New York, 1961) is a concise and sympathetic high-level popularization. Edmund Wilson's *To the Finland Station* (New York, 1940), a literary classic on the history of socialism to 1917, devotes proportionate space to Lenin. A new edition appeared in 1972.

Several collaborative works, topically arranged, have been published in recent years. The most useful is Leonard Schapiro and Peter Reddaway (eds.), *Lenin: The Man, the Theorist, the Leader* (New York, 1967). Bernard W. Eissenstat (ed.), *Lenin and Leninism* (Lexington, Mass., 1971), contains seventeen contributions, most of them rather short pieces. A brief Marxist symposium is Paul Sweezy and Harry Magdoff (eds.) *Lenin Today* (New York, 1970). The standard work on Lenin's ideas is Alfred G. Meyer's *Leninism* (Cambridge, Mass, 1957). See also Michael Morgan's *Lenin* (Athens, Ohio, 1972) on the development of his ideology. Special topics include Anna Rochester, *Lenin on the Agrarian Question* (New York, 1942), a Communist interpretation; Thomas T. Hammond, *Lenin on Trade Unions and Revolution, 1893–1917* (New York, 1957); and Alfred D. Low, *Lenin on the Question of Nationality* (New York, 1958). See also *Lenin: A Study in the Unity of His Thought* (London, 1970) by the Hungarian Marxist George Lukács, essays first published in 1924, and Louis Althusser, *Lenin and Philosophy* (London, 1971).

Regarding primary sources, the quantity is enormous but the quality disappointing. Some of the early recollections are valuable, especially those of Krupskaya, Trotsky, Gorky, and Zetkin. Important reminiscences by Fotieva, Valentinov, and Balabanoff have appeared more recently. (Full citations may be found in the reference notes.) Works published in the Soviet Union during the Stalin era (and many since) must be approached with caution. Several collected editions of memoir literature are available. Probably the most useful is *O Vladimire Ilyche Lenine: Vospominania, 1900–1922 gody* [About Vladimir Ilych Lenin: Recollections, 1900–1922] (Moscow, 1963). The most recent—largely reprinted material otherwise difficult to obtain—is G. Golikov and others (eds.), *Vospominania o Vladimire Ilyche Lenine* (5 vols.; Moscow, 1969–70).

3. LENIN AND RUSSIAN SOCIAL DEMOCRACY

In Lenin's case the distinction between biography and the history of Bolshevism is narrow indeed. Leonard Schapiro's *The Communist Party of the Soviet Union* (2nd ed.; New York, 1971) is the standard historical work on the subject, nearly half of it relevant to Lenin's career. Harold Shukman's *Lenin and the Russian Revolution* (New York, 1967) is an able short study from the beginnings of Russian Marxism to 1917. An older work of the same title by Christopher Hill (London, 1947) is attractively written and even more concise, though with a rather simplistic Marxist point of view. The most comprehensive work on the early years (1890–1903) is Dietrich Geyer's *Lenin in der russischen Sozialdemokratie* (Cologne, 1962). J. L. H. Keep's *The Rise of Social*

[186]   LENIN

Democracy in Russia (Oxford, 1963), an objective scholarly account, carries the story to approximately 1907. More specialized studies of the earliest period include Richard Pipes, *Social Democracy and the St. Petersburg Labor Movement, 1885–1897* (Cambridge, Mass., 1963), the same author's essay on the origins of Bolshevism in Pipes (ed.), *Revolutionary Russia* (Cambridge, Mass., 1968), and Leopold Haimson, *The Russian Marxists and the Origins of Bolshevism* (Cambridge, Mass., 1955). The latter emphasizes ideology and is complemented by Allen K. Wildman's *The Making of a Workers' Revolution: Russian Social Democracy, 1891–1903* (Chicago, 1967), something of a "sociological" approach. See also David Lane, *The Roots of Russian Communism* (Assen, The Netherlands, 1969), on the 1898–1907 period. The years 1904–1905 are covered by Solomon M. Schwarz, then a Bolshevik and later a Menshevik émigré, in *The Russian Revolution of 1905* (Chicago, 1967). On Legal Marxism, consult Richard Kindersley, *The First Russian Revisionists* (Oxford, 1962), and Arthur P. Mendel, *Dilemmas of Progress in Tsarist Russia* (Cambridge, Mass., 1961). Two works by a prominent "Economist" have been edited, together with a lengthy introduction by Jonathan Frankel, in *Vladimir Akimov on the Dilemmas of Russian Marxism, 1895–1903* (Cambridge, Eng., 1969). Theodore Dan's *The Origins of Bolshevism* (London, 1964) is probably the most important Menshevik interpretation. Although Lenin is featured less prominently than the title indicates, Donald W. Treadgold's *Lenin and His Rivals* (New York, 1955) is useful on the period 1898–1906.

The decade of Lenin's second emigration (1907–17) has been less well served by specialists. Alfred Levin's *The Second Duma* (2nd ed.; Hamden, Conn., 1966) is a monograph on the Social Democrats and the "constitutional experiment." A basic primary source is A. Badayev (a Bolshevik deputy), *The Bolsheviks in the Tsarist Duma* (London, n.d.). Alfred Senn's *The Russian Revolution in Switzerland, 1914–1917* (Madison, Wis., 1971) devotes appropriate attention to Lenin and the Bolsheviks.

Several biographies of leading Marxists contribute to an understanding of Lenin and the Social Democratic movement. Perhaps the most valuable in this context is Samuel H. Baron's intellectual biography of the "Father of Russian Marxism": *Plekhanov* (Stanford, Calif., 1963). Isaac Deutscher's monumental study of Trotsky is a contemporary classic despite a Marxist bias that frequently fails to confront the Trotsky mystique. The first volume, *The Prophet Armed* (New York, 1954), breaks off in 1921 and is the most relevant to Lenin's career. Israel Getzler's *Martov* (Cambridge, Eng., 1967) is a careful and dispassionate study of Lenin's Menshevik rival. Struve, a friend in Lenin's youth, is the subject of an outstanding biography (projected in two volumes) : Richard Pipes, *Struve: Liberal on the Left, 1870–1905* (Cambridge, Mass., 1970). None of Lenin's prominent associates (e.g., Zinoviev, Kamenev, and Bukharin) have been the subject of an adequate biography, though Warren Lerner's *Karl Radek* (Stanford, Calif., 1970) is useful. There are, of course, numerous biographies of Stalin, but none are especially pertinent for the pre-revolutionary period. However, see Edward Ellis Smith, *The Young Stalin* (New York, 1967). Bertram D. Wolfe's *The Bridge and the Abyss: The Troubled Friendship of Maxim Gorky and V. I. Lenin* (New York, 1967) is absorbing if somewhat peripheral. Robert H. McNeal's engaging biography of Krupskaya, *Bride of the Revolution* (Ann Arbor, Mich., 1972), sheds new light on Lenin's personal life.

4. THE RUSSIAN REVOLUTION

For a bibliographic discussion, see Robert D. Warth, "On the Historiography of the Russian Revolution," *Slavic Review*, XXVI (June 1967). William Henry Chamberlin's *The Russian Revolution* (2 vols.; New York, 1935) is still the standard work on the revolution and civil war. A paperback edition is available (New York, 1965). Less ambitious surveys of the events of 1917 include Joel Carmichael's *A Short History of the Russian Revolution* (New York, 1964), based to a large extent on N. N. Sukhanov's remarkable first-hand account. (The latter is available in an abridged English translation: *The Russian Revolution, 1917* [2 vols.; London, 1955]). Alan Moorehead's *The Russian Revolution* (New York, 1958) is a readable popularization, widely circulated in paperback, that hews to the "German agent" thesis in regard to Lenin and the Bolsheviks. Leon Trotsky's *The History of the Russian Revolution* (3 vols. in 1; New York, 1936) is a lengthy and brilliant apologia for the Bolshevik cause, a historical classic by any criteria. As with the ticklish subject of Lenin, Soviet historians have been subservient to ideological and political constraints and thus unable to produce an acceptable version (from the standpoint of Western standards of scholarship) of the revolutionary year. See P. N. Sobolev and others (eds.), *History of the October Revolution* (Moscow, 1966), for the current "official" view. Marcel Liebman's *The Russian Revolution* (New York, 1972), a Vintage paperback, is an excellent account provided one accepts the author's Leninist premises. Robert Goldston's *The Russian Revolution* (Indianapolis, 1966) is succinct and elementary (also available in paperback).

Among the more specialized studies on the events of 1917, Marc Ferro's *The Russian Revolution of February 1917* (Englewood Cliffs, N.J., 1972) breaks new ground. George Katkov's *Russia 1917: The February Revolution* (New York, 1967) is a fascinating but unconvinc-

ing pro-monarchist interpretation. In *Prelude to Revolution* (Blooming-
ton, Ind., 1968), Alexander Rabinowitch has examined Bolshevik policy
and the July Days with meticulous scholarship. Robert V. Daniels,
Red October (New York, 1967), has challenged, with some success,
the "accepted" version of the Bolshevik Revolution. See also the essays
by Dietrich Geyer and John Keep in the aforementiond Pipes (ed.),
Revolutionary Russia. Other important works relevant to 1917 have
been omitted as incidental to Lenin's activities.

5. LENIN IN POWER

The most comprehensive history of the early years of the Soviet regime
is Edward Hallett Carr's *The Bolshevik Revolution, 1917–1923* (3 vols.;
New York, 1951–53), part of an impressive multivolume history of Soviet
Russia still in progress. Lenin, who naturally plays a major role, is
treated with sympathetic respect. On political matters, see Leonard
Schapiro, *The Origin of the Communist Autocracy* (Cambridge, Mass.,
1956), a study of the opposition to the Soviet state in its early years
(exclusive of the White movement), and Robert V. Daniels, *The Conscience of the Revolution* (Cambridge, Mass., 1960), a detailed history
of the Communist opposition from 1917 to the 1930s. See also Oliver
H. Radkey's *The Sickle Under the Hammer* (New York, 1963), on the
Socialist Revolutionaries in the first months of Soviet rule. Valuable
monographs on special topics include Oliver H. Radkey, *The Election
to the Russian Constituent Assembly of 1917* (Cambridge, Mass., 1950);
John W. Wheeler-Bennett, *The Forgotten Peace: Brest-Litovsk* (New
York, 1939); Paul Avrich, *Kronstadt 1921* (Princeton, N.J., 1970); and
Sheila Fitzpatrick, *The Commissariat of Enlightenment* (Cambridge,
Eng., 1970), covering the years 1917–21. On Soviet nationality policy
(1917–23), Richard Pipes, *The Formation of the Soviet Union* (2nd
ed.; New York, 1968), is indispensable.

The civil war and Allied intervention (in addition to Soviet diplomacy) has produced an extensive literature of its own, most of it tan-
gential to Lenin's career. The best synthesis of the complicated story of
intervention is John Silverlight, *The Victors' Dilemma* (New York,
1970). The most competent guide to Moscow's diplomacy with the
Allies in 1918–19 is John M. Thompson's *Russia, Bolshevism, and the
Versailles Peace* (Princeton, N.J., 1966). On Soviet-American relations,
see George F. Kennan's *Russia Leaves the War* and *The Decision to
Intervene* (Princeton, N.J., 1956–58), and for Anglo-Soviet relations,
Richard H. Ullman's *Intervention and the War* and *Britain and the
Russian Civil War* (Princeton, N.J., 1963–68). On relations with Ger-
many, Gerald Freund's *Unholy Alliance* (New York, 1957) is probably
the most useful on the period of Lenin's rule. See also Kurt Rosenbaum's

Community of Fate (Syracuse, N.Y., 1965). The Russo-Polish War is treated with scholarly detachment in Piotr S. Wandycz, *Soviet-Polish Relations, 1917–1921* (Cambridge, Mass., 1969). More general histories of Soviet foreign relations include George F. Kennan's interpretive *Russia and the West Under Lenin and Stalin* (Boston, 1961); Louis Fischer's *The Soviets in World Affairs, 1917–1929* (2 vols.; new ed., Princeton, N.J., 1951), still important for the author's unique first-hand sources of information; Adam B. Ulam's analytical and comprehensive *Expansion and Coexistence* (New York, 1968); and Robert D. Warth's narrative treatment, *Soviet Russia in World Politics* (New York, 1963).

On the foundation and early history of the Comintern, James W. Hulse, *The Forming of the Communist International* (Stanford, Calif., 1964), is basic. Other general works include Stanley W. Page, *Lenin and World Revolution* (New York, 1959), and Branko Lazitch, *Lénine et la IIIᵉ internationale* (Paris, 1951). Still of great interest is Franz Borkenau's interpretive *World Communism* (new ed.; Ann Arbor, Mich., 1962), a minor classic originally published in 1939. More specialized works on the major Communist parties (and related material) include Werner Angress, *Stillborn Revolution* (Princeton, N.J., 1963), the best scholarly account of the German party in the early 1920s; Arnold Reisberg, *Lenins Beziehungen zur deutschen Arbeiterbewegung* (Berlin, 1970); Helmut König, *Lenin und der italienische Sozialismus, 1915–1921* (Cologne, 1967); John M. Cammett, *Antonio Gramsci and the Origins of Italian Communism* (Stanford, Calif., 1967); and Robert Wohl, *French Communism in the Making, 1914–1924* (Stanford, Calif., 1966).

The period of Lenin's illness, particularly his "break" with Stalin, is ably and sympathetically discussed in Moshe Lewin, *Lenin's Last Struggle* (New York, 1968). Other helpful works, aside from Lenin biographies, include the second volume of Deutscher's trilogy on Trotsky, *The Prophet Unarmed* (New York, 1959), and several Stalin biographies. Robert D. Warth's *Joseph Stalin* (New York, 1969) is a concise treatment. H. Montgomery Hyde, *Stalin: The History of a Dictator* (New York, 1972) is popular and anecdotal. Robert Payne's *The Rise and Fall of Stalin* (New York, 1965) is sensational and unreliable. Isaac Deutscher's *Stalin: A Political Biography* (2nd ed.; New York, 1967) is "standard" but obsolete for the Lenin-Stalin controversy (the original edition was published in 1949 and not otherwise altered except for updating).

Index

Acton, Lord, 173
Adler, Victor, 81
Agrarian question, 45, 61, 108–109, 119–20; *see also* Peasants
Alexander III, 22, 24
Allied powers, 14, 17, 90, 108, 115, 119, 125, 127, 130, 131, 135
American Relief Administration, 145
Alliluyev, Sergei, 96
Anna Karenina (Tolstoy) , 79
April Theses, 89
Armand, Inessa, 14, 18, 75, 79, 80, 172
Armenia, 151, 161
August Bloc, 76
Austria, 81, 93, 94, 132
Axelrod, Paul, 30, 32, 38, 39, 42, 43, 48, 50, 54
Azerbaizhan, 151

Bakunin, 89
Balabanov, Angelica, 130, 131
Baltic territories, 114
Bavaria, 131, 132
Bazarov, Vladimir, 71
Beethoven, 16
Belgium, 80
Bernstein, Eduard, 37–38, 41, 54, 67
Bibliothèque Nationale, 73
Black Hundreds, 59, 62
Black Sea, 125, 127, 166
Bloody Sunday, 55, 56
Bogdanov, Alexander, 66, 69, 70, 71, 72, 74
Bogdanov, Boris, 89
Bolshevik Military Organization, 104
Bolshevik Revolution, 50, 53, 103, 104, 116, 119, 129, 142, 143, 168

Bolsheviks, Bolshevik party, 13, 14, 52, 58, 60, 64, 66, 71, 77, 87, 91 92, 94, 96, 100, 101, 105, 110, 112, 115, 118, 120, 124, 127, 130; return to Russia, 18; conference, 59, 76, 77, 79, 90, 103; leave Duma, 82; as German "agents," 95; underground, 97; congress, 98; *see also* Social Democratic Labor Party, Communist Party
Bolshevism, 13, 17, 28, 44, 45, 53, 54, 56, 89, 118, 123, 130, 141, 171; *see also* Communism, Communist Party
Bolshoi Theater, 98, 131
Bonapartism, 53, 99
Bonch-Bruyevich, Vladimir, 94, 107, 117
Bosporus, straits of, 90
Brest-Litovsk, 114, 116, 144; treaty of, 116, 123, 135
Brezhnev, Leonid, 170
British Museum, 46, 71
Bukharin, Nikolai, 91, 98, 101, 115, 116, 154, 155, 161, 162, 168
Bund, 50, 51

Canada, 91
Capital (Marx) , 26
Capitalism, 23, 46, 47, 81, 85, 86, 144; Lenin on, 28; Russian, 29, 32
Capri, 71, 72, 74
Central Committee (R.S.D.L.P., Bolshevik Party, Communist Party) , 52, 53, 54, 62, 63, 64, 73, 76, 78, 79, 90, 93, 94, 96, 100, 101, 102, 103, 104, 107, 109, 112, 115, 128, 144, 150, 152, 153, 154, 156, 158, 159, 161, 167, 170